Tenement Press / Harry Caul 1, MMXXV
ISBN 978-1-917304-07-8

SNOW, ALWAYS SNOW

A conversation between Stanley Schtinter & Gareth Evans
on the implications & associations relative to a film
SCHNEEWITTCHEN
(S. Schtinter, 70m, 35mm, MMXXV)

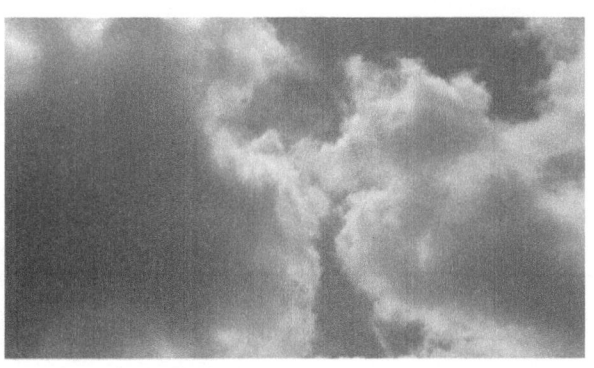

Everything I have neglected to say can be given voice by others.
 —Robert Walser

Stanley Schtinter & Gareth Evans, In Conversation   XIX

Stanley Schtinter, Oversights   LXXXIII

Joshua Bonnetta, Herisau Sketches (October 8)   XCIX

PRINZ	Wie schön du darin lagst. So liegt
	Schnee auf der stillen Winterwelt.

SCHNEEWITTCHEN	Schnee, immer Schnee?

PRINCE   How beautiful you lay therein,
                 snow in a silent winter world.

SNOW WHITE   Snow, always snow?

                     —R.W.

'The visual is essentially pornographic,' wrote Fredric Jameson, adding that 'pornographic films are thus only the potentiation of films in general, which ask us to stare at the world as though it were a naked body.' Turning down the Prince [Toby Jones] and his invitation to watch the passionate lovemaking between the Evil Queen [Julie Christie] and the Hunter [Hanns Zischler], Snow White [Stacy Martin] retorts, 'Rather than look, I'd rather hear.'

Sound supersedes sight in Stanley Schtinter's austere anti-fairy tale SCHNEEWITTCHEN, an English-language remake of João César Monteiro's BRANCA DE NEVE (2000), made largely of an audio performance of Robert Walser's titular play set to a black screen, occasionally relieved by shots of passing clouds. In Walser's radical reworking of the Grimm fable, a resurrected Snow White reconciles with the Evil Queen, denying any foul play and even seeking forgiveness for provoking her jealousy.[*]

A parable for our post-truth times, Schtinter's film provokes reflection on the ontology of a tale as it travels across languages, mediums, geographies and eras. If Walser's play breaks the reader's foundational trust in a benevolent, just world, SCHNEEWITTCHEN breaches the implicit contract with the film spectator, offering a motion picture emptied of both motion and pictures: a work where the visual can only appear as excess.

—Srikanth Srinivasan,
IFFR: International Film Festival
Rotterdam (2024)

*

---

[*] See Robert Walser, (tr) D. Pantano & J. Reidel, 'Schneewittchen' / 'Snow White' in *Fairy Tales: Dramolettes* (New York, NY: New Directions, 2015).

SCHNEEWITTCHEN is a feature film by the artist and author Stanley Schtinter; an auditorium-only, 35mm presentation of which only one print exists.

In what follows, director Stanley Schtinter and producer Gareth Evans consider their collaborative work on SCHNEEWITTCHEN—discuss the project's implications & associations—and consider the film a catalyst fit to enable a wide-ranging conversation. They touch on the water damage done by mainstream culture to our contemporary critical faculty; consider sight and storytelling; imagination and image-making; creativity and light; the luminosity of the dark; and riff on the implications borne by an ownership of the means of production in an age of extinction. A feature-length discussion grounded in their collaboration; their exchange is a commons composed of 18181 words.

*

An abridged iteration of Schtinter and Evans's dialogue was broadcast via the London-based radio station, Resonance 104.4FM, in the days following the film's UK premiere at the British Film Institute, London, 12.02.25, and this volume was produced for the first North American screening of the project at the Anthology Film Archives, 20 / 23.03.25.

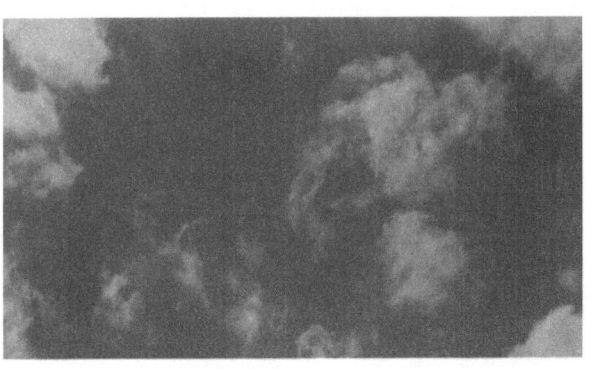

PRINZ [Mein] Ohr wie in der Hängematt'
des Horchens, träumt von Geigenton,
Gelispel, holdem Nacht'gallaut,
von Lieb'sgezwitscher. Hin und her
geht Träumen wie der Wellenschlag
des Sees an unseres Gartens Rand.

PRINCE   My ear hangs rapt on its richness
in a hammock of harkening,
while dreaming of a violin strain,
a lisp, a fair nightingale's song,
of love's twittering. In and out
the dreaming goes like ocean waves
washing onto our garden shore.

—R.W.

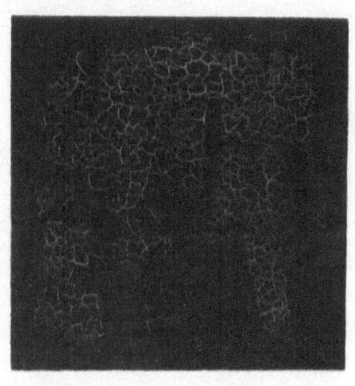

[...]
Kazimir Malevich, Чёрный квадрат / 'Black Square' (1915)

> [...]
> What if the big provocation of *Branca de Neve* would be, alas, there is no provocation at all.
> —Luís Miguel Oliveira, 'No quarto escuro' / 'In the Dark Room,' *João César Monteiro* (2005)

EVANS

Hello and welcome wherever and whenever you are reading this conversation. It's great to be speaking with Stanley Schtinter, someone I know well, someone I've collaborated and worked with a number of times over the years. Schtinter is an artist, writer, curator, a record label owner, a prankster, a provocateur, an interventionist into contemporary culture and society, shaking things up, revealing the hidden, celebrating the underseen and the marginalised.

Stanley, welcome.

SCHTINTER

Gareth Evans, thank you, and for anyone who doesn't know, Gareth is the all too often invisible catalyst making possible countless projects in the culture, like this one, in London and beyond, that even with all of the best intentions and activity, would otherwise not exist. So, praise be.

EVANS

Well, thank you. It's great to be involved and to work with people like yourself and others to make and help these projects wherever possible. I'm delighted today that we're speaking in a slightly different capacity rather than simply in interview, because we're poking the spurs of a project, a very exciting one at that, and one that it has been a great process to work with you on. We're talking here about your new film work, SCHNEEWITTCHEN (2025)—from the fairy tale, the dramatic episode written by Robert Walser.

That's all I'm going to say about it at the moment and I'd like you, if you could, to set the scene as regards the work and also your own impulse to make your filmic version of it.

SCHTINTER

Walser's text is a disenchanted fairytale adaptation that begins where the story of SNOW WHITE, as it is most commonly told, ends. The dwarves are disposed of. The Prince never has his way with Snow, and the poisoning is potentially a practical joke, or indeed a performance, a play. The characters in Walser's telling are afforded agency, and ambivalence, so that they are aware of the roles they are playing, but not so aware that they can change them. The audience condemns the players to repeat their parts. Walser might be quietly asking whether we, the audience, can or should expect much more from our version of reality, if we will not tell better stories.

Whether or not he intended for his SNOW WHITE to be performed is unclear, but it does sit on the page as script. The film uses the text without interference (the sole intervention being Pantano and Reidel's translation of the text into English language). It was translated into Portuguese for João César Monteiro's film, BRANCA DE NEVE, in the year 2000. He, too, used the text unedited, though translated into Portuguese.

Some few years ago, I was looking out over the landscape or hellscape of films being produced for general consumption, with the obvious dominance of remakes and franchise revivals, and I thought: what is the absolute last film that would ever be made in this culture, remade at this moment? And it is surely Monteiro's SNOW WHITE. So, therein lies the first motivation. May this be the last remake.

[...]

Será o luar das vacas
este bafo nocturno
pairando na destruição das vozes?

Este rumor de fantasmas
envenenando a verdade do sangue
será o luar das vacas?
   —João César Monteiro, 'Génesis,'
   Corpo submerso (edição do autor, 1959)

EVANS

That's a great summary, and it's certainly the kind of pitch that you'd initially made to me when you were beginning to think about your own take on this material... To think about how it could be brought about, as you say, in a kind of hellscape where there is choice, yes, there is choice. Certainly, if one goes online, one can find a kind of level field from across the decades of moving image and sound work where everything is equivalent on one level.

At the same time, the journey through that ecotone is almost impossible unless you have some idea of what you're looking at, some form of value system, and a sort of informed method for filtration, should we say. But it's interesting, isn't it? About Walser... He's a Swiss writer—died in 1956, on Christmas Day famously—and died, at that point, certainly in English language terms, essentially unknown to the wider reading community until he was recovered in the early 1980s by the late translator and writer Christopher Middleton, and an important collection called THE WALK (1955).

Walser's work was subsequently picked up by critics, such as Susan Sontag, and moved very quickly into wider circulation in the English-speaking world. Now many, many of his stories, fragments, and microscopic texts are being translated and brought into English, particularly via New York Review Books and New Directions. But the impulse to remake is really interesting, isn't it, because this work that you've made falls into a number of different strands or strains, if you like, of contemporary culture and cinema.

[...]

> In long as in short prose Walser is a miniaturist, promulgating the claims of the anti-heroic, the limited, the humble, the small—as if in response to his acute feeling for the interminable. Walser's life illustrates the restlessness of one kind of depressive temperament: he had the depressive's fascination with stasis, and with the way time distends, is consumed; and spent much of his life obsessively turning time into space: his walks. His work plays with the depressive's appalled vision of endlessness: it is all voice—musing, conversing, rambling, running on. The important is redeemed as a species of the unimportant, wisdom as a kind of shy, valiant loquacity.
> —Susan Sontag, 'Walser's Voice,'
> in Robert Walser, (tr.) C. Middleton,
> *et al*, *Selected Stories* (1982)

I wonder if you could think for us about how and where you would place SCHNEEWITTCHEN as a project, because—I mean, I'll come back to you in a minute with my own thoughts—but I know you have particular ideas as to how the work should be considered before we even get into the details of what it, itself, is. The impulse for you comes perhaps from outside cinema?

SCHTINTER

I understand that the film is likely to be positioned within a certain context or tradition, or my intentions are. This would be the Letterist movement, or Malevich's 'Black Square' (1915) or Derek Jarman's BLUE (1993). But the historical-political and cultural context for me is that of the films that could or could not be made behind the Iron Curtain. In that time and space of censorship, filmmakers were allowed to make only explicit propaganda pieces or fairy tales. I see very little difference today. You can make what you like—to a point—but it won't be seen.

EVANS

Animators, live-action filmmakers like Švankmajer and many others—Borowczyk, et cetera—across the whole of Eastern and Central Europe, were coding ideas into children's material, ostensibly children's material; narratives, ideas, and subversive positions that the authorities just completely ignored because they thought that the children's space was somehow one outside of which such messages could be carried or would even be noticed. And yet ironically, those societies were extremely aware educationally; of the official classroom, shall we say; of the culture and the society of forms of indoctrination from the earliest age. It's very interesting that you see that line that you feel part of, that the educational space when it's officially declared is, you know, one of control.

Whereas the education that most of us get comes from outside of the classroom in life and experience and relationships and social understanding. And just before we started this conversation, we were talking about text that you're not allowed to bring into English classrooms anymore, even if you're a formally qualified teacher teaching the curriculum, text that might speak to an Anti-capitalist position now in 2024 in the UK. I think it was very canny of you to actually realise that the remake culture that you're challenging is also one in which forms of learning and knowledge exchange and information and awareness about the societal and political implications of the way we live can come very, very strikingly through what is ostensibly material for younger people.

I'm thinking back now to what you did with IMPORTANT BOOKS (2021–2022), your audio anthology of manifestos read by children, I think all under the age of twelve. Were you thinking of this project as a kind of sequel to that in a different medium? I say this as we've not yet spoken directly to the nature of this project on screen, but—of course—the 'sonic' is absolutely central to it.

SCHTINTER

I hadn't made that connection consciously, but the realisation of IMPORTANT BOOKS (OR, MANIFESTOS READ BY CHILDREN) —was motivated by the British government's decision during Covid-19 to secret in a new law preventing teachers from using materials in schools that 'express a wish to end Capitalism.' [See Mattha Busby, 'Schools in England told not to use material from Anti-capitalist groups,' *The Guardian*, 27.09.20.] And so, when we're talking about that moment, behind the Curtain, I think it's useful to think about what children's materials are today, how they are repackaged and to what end.

SCHNEEWITTCHEN is reactive, as was IMPORTANT BOOKS. Government and corporation use advanced forms of manipulation and censorship as they always have done, but I wonder if they've ever been so considerably in lockstep with, or, in the possession of, such intelligent private interests? Interests that derive profit from making us stupid. And I mean really stupid. And it's hard to imagine a way out of this, given how completely locked-in every one and thing has become. We no longer possess autonomous items—be it a book or a hammer—that you can share. Instead, you, the individual, have to subscribe; such a logic dictates that whatever you do, and wherever you go, is on record. I don't know what word to give this, but I know that the principle of it is the opposite of freedom. Everything is software, and the programme is closed. Be it a synthesiser or a motorcycle engine: you can no longer intervene. You can no longer look beneath the hood and begin to understand for yourself its inner-workings and adapt them to your preference. We live, all of us, day-by-day, according to what any culture before ours would recognise as magic, and a black magic at that.

This kind of liberated totalitarianism, paradoxical as that sounds, is a long time coming. Rousseau predicted and advocated for the tyranny of overseeing and oversharing, suggesting that people would censor themselves if they were constantly exposed. That is what the digital has done.

[...]

Imagination no longer comes as cheaply as it did in the past. The slightest move in the virtual landscape has to be paid for in lines of code.
—Bruno Latour, 'Beware, Your Imagination Leaves Digital Traces,' *The Times Literary Supplement* (2006)

SCHNEEWITTCHEN is analogue in its making and its presentation. This isn't fetishist nor reactionary, but a temporary escape from the horror I've described; an attempt to open and share in some kind of hidden place.

In a recent screening, the great American independent film director (and cinematographer *par excellence*) Sean Price Williams, said that the experience reminded him of being lulled to sleep as a child, as regards the stories that we're told, and critically the way that we are (and have) told them.

At the risk of digressing, I saw WONKA (2024) the other day. I went with my mother, because she complained—and it is true—that we never do anything together. The other films showing at that cinema seemed all the worse, and so, WONKA.

Perhaps I have a sugar-coated recollection of the original film (CHARLIE & THE CHOCOLATE FACTORY, 1971), but it seems to me that everything from the name outwards is innuendo. It is strange and threatening. I think these qualities, and the ambiguity of the protagonist / antagonist's character focus a child's developing mind. Wonka is the conjurer of the magic, of the sweetness, and he is not to be trusted. Charlie's inheritance from Wonka is established through disobedience: through questioning the illusion. He is the only one who sees through it, the only one who isn't tricked.

This franchise revival removes any tension, or threat. Moreover, it removes disobedience. It removes magic! It is pure confection, rather than [sic] 'Pure Imagination,' but that confection is so impure that even the chocolate looks completely inedible.

    Meanwhile, in present time, the long-standing adultification of the child and paedofilification of the female form in visual culture has now apparently extended to the male. The muscular is implicitly dangerous, and the ambiguities that form *character*, which captivate and enrich their audience, are effectively forbidden. In the 70s, our sleuth hero was the fat drunk—and the thin drunk before him in the 50s and the 60s—and then we got Arnold Schwarzenegger, with a brief respite in the brawny funny-man, Bruce Willis. Now? Now you will get the angrogyne-skinnymalinky Timothy Chalamet; you will get nothing, and you will be grateful.

    What actually wounded me about WONKA is that the dir-ector's previous movie was PADDINGTON (2014). Everybody loved that film, and sometimes, incredibly—as was the case with THE SOPRANOS (1999-2007)—everybody wasn't wrong. THE PADDINGTON adaptation was deployed in the wake of Brexit, and it seemed to attempt to confront the nastier edges of what provoked people to vote as they did. Paddington is forced to leave his home because it is no longer tenable to live there. He is a refugee. And this, though a child's movie, is performed without infantilising its audience or cheapening—monetising—the experience of the person (or in this case the symbolic, speaking bear) fleeing.

EVANS

There is an expectation of a certain kind of making in films such as WONKA and in PADDINGTON, and were you to push an element within that, the structure is strong enough to hold it for those who only want to see the established position, shall we say, in either case. I think of that because of the sheer strength of the established position, the familiarity of those structures that support it. One—a maker, an interventionist of some kind—can enter that space and locate and secrete other stories and other messages. It's really interesting. And I think you're doing that here with SNOW WHITE—with SCHNEEWITTCHEN—as the story is so given a part of our global culture. 2025 is the year of the Disney remake of their own SNOW WHITE, which they arguably could claim is the one that will be taken as reference point for this story, which is what gives your own project even more urgency.

But what I like about the PADDINGTON / WONKA connection is that you're making an alliance, if you like, between certain projects where something is so seen, has been so overseen, that it needs a response... a reaction either from within, something near-sighted, or from elsewhere. Now you perform both, I think—per SNOW WHITE—and I'd like to stay with the sonic if we could, and talk about the sound design, the scoring. But first of all, we should touch on the voices we hear in the film, the voices of the five characters.

Tell us, first of all, who the cast are, and what—for you—their casting does for this work, because it seems to me that it's the game changer for this project. It's what is distinct, what makes it distinctive as regards other forms of canon challenging intervention, shall we say?

[...]
> A garden. To the right the palace entrance. In the
> background rolling mountains. The Queen, Snow
> White, the foreign Prince, the Hunter.
> —Robert Walser, (tr.) D. Pantano & J. Reidel,
> 'Snow White,' *Komödie: Märchenspiele
> und szenische Dichtungen / Fairy Tales:
> Dramolettes* (1986 / 2015)

SCHTINTER
In SCHNEEWITTCHEN—
in the role of the Queen, Julie Christie;
in the role of the Hunter, Hanns Zischler;
in the role of the King, Stephen Dillane;
the Prince is Toby Jones;
and Snow White is played by Stacy Martin.

EVANS
First of all, it was a great result to be able to work with such talents, all of whom bring remarkable things both in their own performances but also in the inheritance(s) that they bring to this work from all their other works in multiple (and multiple means multiple; multiple media and across multiple platforms). I guess, for me, what makes it so exciting is—in a way—what we've just been talking about: about the idea of working with

performers who have been overseen by the culture, in different ways; both overseen in terms of a sense of power (to a certain degree), but also whom have been seen too much or too much in a certain way.

So, Julie Christie—one of the icons of 20th century cinema—whose own first lead role saw her win the Academy Award for Best Actress with DARLING (1965), a film about a woman who is herself overseen and who is both destructive and destroyed...

At the other end of the spectrum, age-wise—sixty years on from DARLING, more or less—Stacy Martin makes her debut in NYMPHOMANIAC (2013), Lars von Trier's exploration of the pornographic imagination and the overseen nature of visual physicality. We have an interesting dynamic there, with the female cast, but at the same time, the male performers all have versions of the overseen within them. Stephen Dillane is perhaps most well-known to global audiences as one of the key protagonists in GAME OF THRONES (2011–2019), the great spectacle of the television broadcast age. Toby Jones is now overseen in a sense—in a very good way, one would argue—as one of the UK's national treasures, and Hanns Zischler, while perhaps less familiar to British audiences, is absolutely a given to any cinephile who's listening because he is one of the great double acts in Wim Wender's KINGS OF THE ROAD (1976), driving his Volkswagen into the lake at the beginning of the film.

So, you've assembled an incredible cast who are not seen in your work, and that, I think, is already creating an incredible tension with the history of cinema, with the history of performative drama, whether on screen or on the radio, and challenges the idea of what makes and gives a work status when status is attached to that work by other means.

I think that's one of the many things that made it very exciting for me to work with you on this project. Let's stay with the sound, could we—or the heard, should we say—and tell us about the sound design and the scoring?

SCHTINTER

I don't know whether I made this up, but I'm sure that an old employee at Close-Up Film Centre had once described Julie Christie entering the venue, disguised, taking out a membership—renting Monteiro's BRANCA DE NEVE—and never returning to the venue, never returning the disc. It's something I only remembered much later. It wasn't conscious when I approached Julie, or during the making, but it was evidently there somewhere. I hope she'll forgive my tabloid slant to the days before the snowfall.

The sound design and the scoring are one. Both have been composed and assembled by Joshua Bonnetta, who is not a formally trained sound designer—whatever that means. He is an artist in the most profound sense of the word: capital A. A*. Easter Island. Full marks. Off the chart. SOLAR. His ability to move seamlessly from the crickets of the Amazon to Siberian snowfall is where I hoped he would locate this Snow White. And he did. I'm conscious of how much we should speak to the assembly, though—its constituent parts—because this is not a film that is going to be accessed with the same ease that other films are.

As long as I have power over it, which ought to be life-long because this is an entirely independent production, it will not be sold. It will not be streamed online, nor will it be available digitally. (I have considered a single exception, the Spring Equinox, because that is—accidentally or otherwise—when Disney will officially release theirs, but I think any digital distribution is very unlikely.) It is an event that people have to travel to, made very explicitly for auditorium playback.

Monteiro called his film an open path, or an asshole. If his film was looking at the void, then mine intends to be the void staring right back at it.

EVANS

I think it's very important that you've mentioned that it will not be streamed, that the work will not be available digitally. That it'll only be available in an event capacity in the public space, however that public space is defined. I say this in terms of the ideas of meeting and paying attention, as we remember from the great Simone Weil who'd said, 'attention is prayer.'

[...]
Attention, taken to its highest degree, is the same thing as prayer. It presupposes faith and love.
Absolutely unmixed attention is prayer.
—Simone Weil, (tr.) E. Crawford & M. von der Ruhr, 'Attention & Will,' *La Pesanteur et la Grace / Gravity & Grace* (1947 / 2002)

This seems to me to be absolutely central to what you're trying to do here, highlighting the nature of the elements that make up cinema in a reflexive way... I mean, it seems very important to underscore this aspect without necessarily explaining again the distinction between that which is inside and outside the work, but that you are—at every point—drawing attention to the mechanics and motivations and means by which cinema arrives at our attention, it seems to me, and that's very important. We were talking a little bit earlier about the idea of the voices and the unseen and—in many ways—not just this conversation but also the work itself could be labelled as a sonic or radio work. We're just over a century on from the first radio drama, the first of which being a BBC broadcast, and so there's now a hundred years behind that tradition. How we term the project is very important, as it seems to me to dictate how certain people will receive it. They'll want some signage, they'll want some labelling, and—rightly—you resisted that earlier on in the conversation, just as you challenged the kind of lineage in moving image terms for the work.

In 2025, we're looking at a year in which Disney releases its own live action remake of SNOW WHITE; how would you ideally like this work to circulate, your own work—SCHNEEWITTCHEN—and Disney's project?

SCHTINTER

I'd meant to mention earlier that another motivation for SCHNEEWITTCHEN's making was Disney's own live-action remake of the 1937 film. This was meant to be released in 2023, and then in '24, and now, finally, it's slated for release in '25. It is curious that we have legitimately—and without intention—mirrored their setbacks in our own production schedule.

Disney have copyrighted the words SNOW and WHITE in combination for any recorded media. I don't know whether that extends to SCHNEEWITTCHEN. Who cares. It is a translation of a Portuguese work after the movement of the German original into English, and so to call this work by the original word, in the original romance language, given Walt's possession... There is a bit of a gag there.

The eventual rollout of SCHNEEWITTCHEN, though limited by the nature of our limitations in the one 35mm print, will overlap and compete with the Disney version. I wonder which is likely to boast more walkouts?

How many members of the audience did we lose at the festival premiere at Rotterdam? A quarter? Afterwards, I was approached by a psychotherapist who explained to me what she believed this meant, that 'the film brings people into focus with themselves. It is quite literally a black mirror and that is intolerable and so they have to go.'

[...]

In the mirror I saw that between us and ourselves there is a small gap, a delay that can be measured exactly by the amount of time it takes us to recognise our own image. That miniscule opening gives rise, along with the whole of psychology, to all our neuroses and fears, all the triumphs and failures of the ego. Had we recognised ourselves immediately, had there not been that fleeting intermission, we would be like the angels, entirely devoid of psychology. And we would be bereft of the novel, which narrates [...] the time it takes characters to recognise and misrecognise, to avow and disavow, themselves.
—Giorgio Agamben, (tr.) A.L. Price,
*Quel che ho visto, udito, appreso... /
What I saw, heard, learned...* (2025)

Our reductive, soundbite times have reduced our understanding of the gaze to one particular misreading of a reading. We think about the gaze as something necessarily exploitative, but gaze is also where contemplation happens, and that is the antithesis of the TikTok-ification of visual culture, which is where SCHNEE-WITTCHEN wants to locate itself. At the same time, there is a tension, or perhaps a paradox, in that the film also intends to be a very literal Americanisation of the Portuguese film.

EVANS

I think it's very interesting what you say about Americanisation; about the idea of removing barriers to that encounter in certain ways, toying with the idea of standardisation and reinforcing such barriers, while—at the same time—the film contains all sorts of challenges to conventional cinematic engagement, which the psychotherapist you spoke to identified... the deep root cause of which is powerful and profound. We're not going to talk about all the elements of the work, but I would like to just mention the camera. I think it's very important how you use these brief glimpses of sky in the work because... Well, for two reasons really.

One, they're shot by Sean Price Williams, who is known for his mobile verité—his engaged, fluid, and freewheeling style—and yet here he's obviously asked to contain himself to frame the sky; to allow the movement to take place within the image, as opposed to move with it and / or alongside it. That seems to me to be very powerful, reminding us of the ultimate cinema of the sky itself.

Second, it makes me think of James Turrell's sky spaces, where we're given a framed portion of sky, and allowed to contemplate much larger questions through that lens... You seem to achieve something similar, in two really interesting ways. First, with the presentation of the sky itself, and second—of course—with the absence of sky and image. Both become spaces of meditation.

[...]
Light knows when you're looking.
—James Turrell, *The Guardian* (2015)

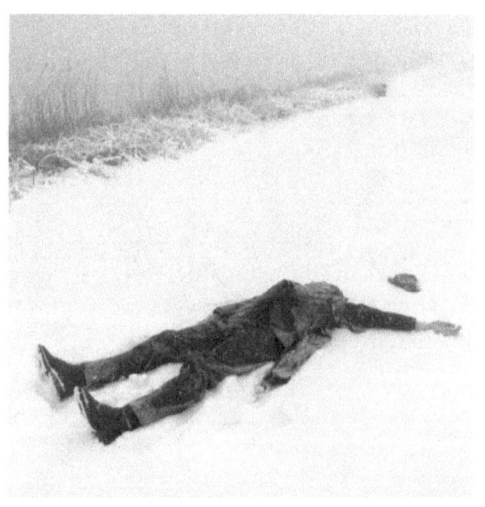

[...]
Stanley Schtinter, *Schneewittchen* (2025)

EVANS

I'd also like to ask you a little bit about your adaptation of the opening image from Monteiro's BRANCA DE NEVE, because that change seems to me to go to the heart of what this project is fundamentally doing and working with at its baseline. In Monteiro's film, its opening image is that of Robert Walser's body. Could you let us know how you amended that?

SCHTINTER

When the author was found on that day, dead in the snow, he was photographed. This was a police formality, rather than the image being taken because he'd been a famous writer. This series of photographs approaching the body, and focussing on the contorted face, deprived of the writer, deprived of the man... At the beginning of Monteiro's film we are forced to look at these. In my film they're replaced by somebody playing dead. That somebody is me, but this isn't a comment on authorship, or vainglorious in some way, but rather of necessity: we had just half a day in Siberia to do it, and Peter Dinklage didn't show up.

EVANS

Exactly, and I think that—whether Dinklage or yourself—the crucial thing is that it's a performance as opposed to an actual image of mortality which, as you've said elsewhere, is a cursed artefact, and I agree.

[...]

> The trope of distant tribespeople, or fire-men, instinctively resisting the camera in 'first contact' with it—fearing that the snap of the photograph would break or steal some essential part of them—is oft-repeated without vindication. But they were, of course, right. They were the last, after all. From man's attempts to influence the hunt to man's insistence on controlling the light, the black magic of the black mirror has smartened and strengthened, tethered as audiences have become to the technologies that in recording experience precisely remove it.
> —Stanley Schtinter, *Last Movies* (2023)

This is where the film makes a huge leap forward in terms of its reach and resonance, it's 'right now,' because we are receiving images of the dead on a 24/7 scale into our pockets; into our hands; onto our phones... Images of a catastrophic assault on a territory where there is no escape, and in which the people are reduced—at best—to numbers and—at worst—not even acknowledged by wider elements of the global media and political culture of our time. These people are effectively unseen or, even if seen, that seeing brings no value, worth, or importance to their life, and now their death.

I think the fact that you have not shown the original image is extremely important. There is a great concern amongst serious, committed, and progressive voices regarding images of death circulating now in contemporary media, and I think that you've challenged that fundamentally. The idea of the unseen and the heard or unheard—which is what this project is finally about or, rather, comes from, explores, and interrogates—is really, really critical.

I'd like to add another thought about the sky. The sky as a roof or ceiling. I mean, the orders of sky that you present to us are the cinema—the roof, the ceiling over all of us, over all of our lives on this planet—and the sky in your film is calm, quiet, and yet there are these acoustical storms that run through the work. These storms—this troubled weather, should we say—is heard alongside and within the human voices of the drama, and it seems to me this is absolutely right. The humans make the storm. The storm is their emotional engagement in relation to each other; their conflicts, their hierarchies, their struggles for power, et cetera. In this way, the film is also an ecological film, it seems to me, because the ecological crisis we find ourselves in is one made and manufactured by human intervention, human activity, and yet—again—it is a crisis denied, unseen, and unheard despite all evidence to the contrary by those in power—like Gaza—and those representing us in power. So, again, it seems to me that this is a work that is absolutely necessary and urgent for our time because it speaks to that void—as you mentioned, the void of the culture; the void looking back at us—but also to what imagination, in the unseeing and unhearing, allows us to encounter. The space that attention brings about, and the flourishing of possibility—both creatively and politically—that the removal of elements brings to us. Gives to us. I would put it into a productive tradition. I mean, I love your alignment with

Eastern and Central European works in different media, but I also think it's a productive operation to think about it as within the counter canon of cinema. Films like Chris Marker's LA JETÉE (1962), in its use of photography; as in Guy Debord's films, and their playing with sound and silence; Warhol's durational and still image films; Jarman's BLUE, as you've already mentioned; or Douglas Gordon's 24-HOUR PSYCHO (1993), slowing a film down so that it becomes kind of granular in its attention...

> [...]
> Consciousness is exhausted. Back now to inorganic matter. This is what we want. We want to be stones in a field.
> —Don DeLillo, *Point Omega* (2010)

We talked about how and where and when SCHNEEWITTCHEN may circulate, and I think if we could perhaps now talk about what it's meant to you to make it, and whether some of the lessons you've learned from it have informed how you might make moving image work in the future?

SCHTINTER

The skies you speak of are silenced. About two thirds of the way through Monteiro's film, there is an additional shot: a tracking camera smoothly surveys the foundations of the mosque upon which Lisbon's Catholic cathedral are built. In SCHNEEWITTCHEN, I didn't try to replicate this, because it isn't very American to reveal the Moslem, or gypsy, or even Jewish foundations. As we've already discussed: the deceased are not to be put on show.

I am trying to come to terms with the motivations for people circulating images of the dead, particularly murdered Palestinians. Children. Defenders of this would reasonably argue that it is because the IDF won't allow reporters into the Gazan territory, or because the Western media are not enough engaged, or at all engaged, with the Palestinian perspective. And while I choose not to participate in anti-social media, I know people who do, who have been contacted as to 'why they aren't posting on Gaza.' A generous read of this is in the desperation and the powerlessness people feel about this appalling situation. A less charitable read is snuff. These corpses are not given voice by the recirculation on one of Mark Zuckerberg's crack-cocaine modelled interfaces, on a consumer device made by slaves intended to generate profit out of the user's free labour. And it isn't all on Zuck and the other tech overlords. People choose this poison, elect to participate, and it has nothing to do with anyone else, but themselves; their arrogant conception of self and success, and the relative protection it provides from the unpredictability of real, lived experience.

The othering of the deceased people is enhanced by those sharing their images alongside their selfies of their East London life of supposed activism, prosecco and Etsy. They are doing the opposite of what they think they're doing. It is inconceivable that a British body would be displayed like this in present time in any circumstances. Or indeed an Israeli one. Not one photograph of a murdered Jew from November 7 has been circulated in the same way. Not one Briton from any of the ISIS attacks in previous years. Racist, obscene, snuff.

In Australia today—and fuck me if I'm holding that place up as any kind of political example, as terminally underrated for its beauty as it is (the aboriginal people are devastated by our inability to hear the stars)—there is a trigger warning any time a dead body is shown on television because, to the people who've been there longer than the white settlers, it is cursed. And of course it is cursed! The camera is perhaps the best we've got, but it's also black magic. Kenneth Anger considered it inherently evil, and I think he has a point.

[...]
I have always considered movies evil; the day that cinema was invented was a black day for mankind.
—Kenneth Anger, as told to
Tony Rayns (1969)

Sometimes good and evil are useful ways of looking at things, as long as we stay close to the reality of this world in shades of grey. To finish, as I've said before: those people who encountered the camera, and feared that it would steal some essential part of them? They were right.

EVANS

That is really striking. True. I think that with indigenous responses to the camera they're not saying that death doesn't matter; it's the opposite. They're saying it matters profoundly, and your recording of it—or one's image capture thereof—is a transgression of a border. Is against the respect that the body demands and needs at that point... I think you're absolutely right and, again, it goes back to what we were saying earlier, as regards the imaginative power of removing the image, the empathetic power that act of removal brings about, as you've just so strongly described, but also—and crucially—the paying of attention that the removal of the image brings regardless of the nature of the image that is then being described. Attention is among the casualties here: proper attention, in the terms of lived experience being brought to the encounter with the subject in question, whatever it might be—on whatever platform—and so I don't think it's wrong of you to make such claims for the work.

It comes from a dramatic response to the SNOW WHITE story; it comes from responses by yourself, Walser and Monteiro to a story that has become a given in Western culture, and yet one that has also been massively abused and appropriated by various forces for commodity gain and profitable recourse. So that's where it comes from, but what a work can do is something altogether different based on the context into which it emerges, the time in which it emerges, and the intentions of the maker in relation to its encounter with an audience. I think that's exactly what's happening here. I think people who have seen the film in whatever context as a kind of a thinning out of source material are completely missing the point as regards what this project actually is. It's an amplification of its source material towards very different ends—more distinctive, maybe, than some of its involved makers have seen because of the time in which it's shown—and so the fact of imagination, the fact of attention, and the priority you give to those two elements is key.

Arguably, the most important elements in our encounter with any artwork are the elements that have been overlooked already by some respondents to this work. Without which —without imagination and attention—we have no art or culture, and I think—as you say—that the process that led to your making comes exactly from your observation that those two elements are almost non-existent now in corporate commodity production. That's why we can make such claims for this work. If other people don't see that, well that's where the conversation can start, and we'll see what happens. Let's make this relation to the nature and purpose of art; to the divine and its relationship to the body; to the treatment of coverage of Gaza; and to the ecological crisis. Let's do that. Let's put it out there that that's what art is for; to make certain claims and then, obviously, if someone challenges and disagrees with those claims, then we'll talk about it. We won't initiate an armed onslaught on that person, we will talk to them. We'll try and bridge that divide of opinion, if there is one. Find a workable solution that can take us all forwards in a shared space. That's why I think this work matters.

And this makes me think again of walking out. I mean, in the culture in which we find ourselves, walking out on the possibility of such a conversation is one of the few actions and gestures left, isn't it? Left to consumers primarily, rather than audiences or viewers or listeners...

In a culture composed of wall-to-wall over-saturation, to leave—to choose to leave a space of consumer cultural presence—is a significant thing. You could argue that most people don't have the chance to actually leave something because they're not involved long enough to actually take part in it and for their leaving to be noticed as a gesture or an act.

In this regard, TikTok is the kind of pinnacle of contemporary culture in all sorts of ways, or the aspiration of so much culture; there's not time enough to leave, because it's over before you've even had the thought to do so. In a way, I think, to actually leave an event, leave a cinema screening in this case, is significant. I mean, we could argue or speculate as to why people are leaving and what they're headed towards outside the auditorium doors, but I think the act of leaving, as we've always spoken about, suggests a response. The passivity of sitting through something without in any way allowing it to get to you, or taking its ideas forward when you leave, or thinking about what you've seen or witnessed or experienced or listened to... In that context, leaving becomes actually a rather positive gesture, because it means that you've been touched, you know, tinted at a level beyond conscious control by what you've just encountered.

I'm sort of in favour of leaving in that respect. Not that I'm encouraging it, you know—and not specifically in relation to SCHNEEWITTCHEN, but—generally—what people are used to consuming in that space now, they aren't touched, they don't have any kind of response, it seems to me. We're not given material that seeks to evoke any real and lasting response.

SCHTINTER

Exactly. We're given content in order to not evoke any response.

Even before the first frame of the film, in present time, warnings to cover every possible interpretation are boldly stated. Threat is the one that I find most interesting, because it suggests an implication rather than rather than anything actually, definitely there... While the fact that mainstream visual kultur thrives on unrelenting depictions of violent death is one invariably shrugged off. The disposability of life. The body count of cinema. The omnipotence of this; of the banality and self-service of visual kultur, has irrevocably changed my experience of being in the cinema. When I go there now, it is the pause that I value. Just being there suspends me from the assault that's going on outside, like a secret garden or the Catholic's great cathedral. What I actually see is very often secondary. The impossibility of pulling out your phone, of being reachable in any way (all the better if you leave your phone at home and travel the city by foot to get where you are going, alone). I am visited then by the muse, however lofty and pretentious that sounds, no matter: it is the space in which I am able to conceive of new ideas, and process things too, about my life, often subconsciously, but I leave to notice that the work has been done.

What bothers me about the walk-out is that the first thing someone is likely to do on leaving the auditorium, just as most people check their phone first thing in the morning and last thing at night, is pull out the device and tune back in to more of the same consensual hallucination. There's no chewing over of the WHY and the WHAT of their leaving. No generative anger, or despair, or delight in getting out.

EVANS

No, that's a really crucial point.

I'm not advocating for walking out as a strategy in relation to SCHNEEWITTCHEN, or generally as regards anything to which great love and effort and concern and care and creative vision have been applied at all. But I just think, in a way... I'm reminded of several things. One such thing is an idea that Michael Haneke expressed. It was a DVD extra; one of those short kind of 10-minute interviews. On the DVD, there's a short interview with him, just about some of the office stuff concerning the film, and then at some point he says, 'Most films are designed to be forgotten as soon as the audience leaves the cinema.' It's always stayed with me. I mean, it's like twenty years now since I'd first heard that. And it's just really stayed with me. What does it mean? There's a huge question inside that single sentence statement—that a product is so packaged—and it goes for art house and world cinema as much as anything else, anything more explicitly commercial.

Whichever artwork we're talking about, or whichever genre, they all have their own tropes—they deploy them more or less skilfully—but they are all, in end, tropes nonetheless. However, an exception: the microscopic handful of works that just refuse any such engagement, works that can't be seen to in turn join a new set of left field tropes, because all those works are fundamentally different from each other. It seems to me, I'm certain, that such works come from a completely different place. A place not just outside of industrial cinema—or, you know, commercial funding or even independent funding models—but they just come from a place that isn't really necessarily even cinema. And I would certainly put this work—SCHNEEWITTCHEN—into such a category.

[...]

种   Editor's Note: The transcription software initially tooled to inform a first draft of this manuscript mistook something spoken for this Chinese character at this precise juncture in the dialogue. Pronounced /chóng/, the character translates into the English language as follows:

Noun	1. Kind
	2. Seed
Verb	1. Plant
	2. Grow

We have preserved the place of this glitch within the text as its definition, deliberate or no, felt pertinent to the direction of traffic.

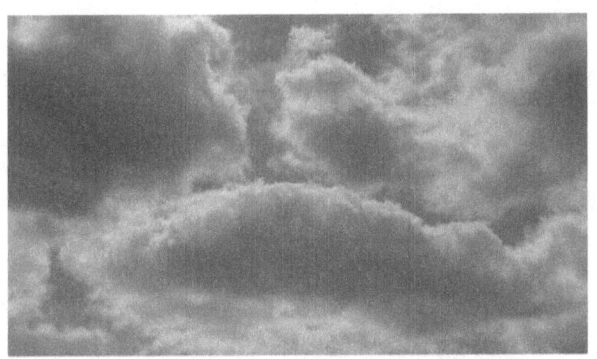

[...]
Stanley Schtinter, *Schneewittchen* (2025)

Obviously, as regards SCHNEEWITTCHEN, it is a cinematic experience we're talking about. Akin to the TURIN HORSE (2011), to SÁTÁNTANGÓ (1994)—to Michael Snow's WAVELENGTH (1967), or a whole load of other examples across a history of cinema... Works that simply refuse any associative lineage. It's the ramifications that are important, and this is very, very [Again, this emphasis is a machine intervention, as opposed to words from Evans's own, palpable mouth; it has been maintained herein because what Evans is saying is important.] significant. Alchemical, even.

Another point I'd like to raise is prompted by something I've read more recently in *Brick*—the Canadian arts and literary journal—wherein I'd found this short piece about moments in cinema that don't officially mean anything, and yet poetically attached themselves to your consciousness... The point in the image that draws attention, regardless of whether it's the official focus or not.

> [...]
> What does my body know of Photography? I observed that a photograph can be the object of three practices (or of three emotions, or of three intentions): to do, to undergo, to look.
> —Roland Barthes, (tr.) R. Howard, *La Chambre claire : Note sur la photographie / Camera Lucida: Reflections on Photography* (1980 / 1981)

Those moments which are expressively resonant and yet—if you try to attach meaning to them within the unfolding narrative of the film—you fail. They don't mean anything as such, independently, but they absolutely add to the tone, texture, depth, timbre of a scene and, ultimately, the film.

There's one such moment they'd mentioned.

Two characters are standing at the edge of a bridge or a quayside, or such like, and one of them kicks a small bottle —a beer bottle or similar—off the edge, and it's night, and we wait for a while, and then the bottle hits the earth, the rocks below. You can try and attach meaning to this instance—something per the fragility of life, or the vulnerability of one of the characters in the scene and the narrative, whatever—but, ultimately, you can't. Such connotations are fruitless.

You can *try*, however, and—in trying—you're breathing; there's a kind of breathing exercise innate to such thinking; but what you can't deny is that the scene took your attention.

This is something outlawed in almost all commercial and independent art house and world cinema work now. It's historical. You know, consider the Golden Age of Americana, where you'd watch an actor brushing their teeth for half an hour, and you just want them to go on forever; or wonderful details from Film Noir, in so-called B-movies of the 40s and 50s, where these kinds of detail constantly emerge... This leads me on to responding to your point about administrative space. I think the primary quality of cinema—cinema in the way that you're describing it —is exactly because of these kinds of moments. It's exactly those details that make cinema a space, nothing to do with narrative or character depth, I think. However sophisticated, it's those moments which ultimately are beyond meaning that spike something.

The fact that SCHNEEWITTCHEN doesn't have an image sequence or allow for such moments to arise has nothing to do with its capacity to contribute to this train of thought.

The sky as seen inside the film provides you with a moment of pause or punctuation between scenes. The images you provide are huge anchors of relation for the viewer, for the listener, and crucially—in the constancy of the pitch-black screen—there's always the possibility that an image might emerge, but you don't quite know. Although one might watch two or three scenes and establish that there's a slither of sky between them, the film is unstable enough—uncertain enough in its authorship—that we cannot be certain. This fact is, potentially, one of the many things that might keep a viewer in their seat as opposed to walking but, crucially, it kind of charges you, it seems to me. It fuels the viewer to move, gives them literally a kind of energy, to move into the idea and the acceptance of

SCHNEEWITTCHEN as a film that could generate these kinds of moments. That breath. Hence, it becomes meditative in the way that you describe.

Now, I'm not saying you can't meditate in PADDINGTON IN PERU (2024), of course you can, but I think the quality of anticipation is very different in such a case. You start with an intention, with focus, and that qualifies attention; an attention to (and the intention of) the work are aspects more or less likely to encourage a certain response. I think that you definitely and explicitly have encouraged a reflective response, an immanent response, because you have removed the image. By definition, everyone's psychic encounter with the work, for the vast majority of its running time, will be their own. A singular one.

The castle, the words, the rain—the distant sounds, et cetera—they're all there, and take us back to the very beginnings of storytelling, The voice around the campfire regaling us with actions and events that come out of a darkness that surrounds them almost entirely. Such a tradition is mirrored in SCHNEEWITTCHEN... The darkness therein is historical, dressed in fear and threat. The stories that we think about in the context of such a sort of speculative space—those of an absent image revealed in the dark—they are all directly, almost biologically linked. It is not just because SCHNEEWITTCHEN is a Grimm tale, but they're connected in much deeper conceptual terms. The tissue of storytelling itself. The idea that the story, as a form, is a response, a softening, an act of calming and taming an incipient darkness.

SCHTINTER
However much I want to, I have resisted establishing a clandestine, autonomous network abbreviated to FFS (the Free Fire Society), for fear of its widespread misinterpretation as a call to random acts of arson. But ultimately and truly, in filmmaking and in film programming, that is the return I'd like to make: to fire, the original screen, and us lot freely interpreting and sharing our stories around it. It'll happen again, no doubt, except that I'm haunted by the story of the islanders who, for a good few hundred years, owing to an eternal flame that was accidentally extinguished, actually forgot how to make fire. (There was of course a terrible poetry recently in David Lynch walking out on us with the great fires of Hollywood.)

[...]
The screen is not a frame like that of a picture
but a mask which allows only a part of the action
to be seen. When a character moves off screen,
we accept the fact that he is out of sight, but he
continues to exist in his own capacity at some other
place in the decor which is hidden from us. There
are no wings to the screen. There could not be
without destroying its specific illusion, which is
to make of a revolver or of a face the very centre of
the universe. In contrast to the stage the space
of the screen is centrifugal. It is because that infinity
which the theatre demands cannot be spatial that
its area can be none other than the human soul.
Enclosed in this space the actor is at the focus of
a two-fold concave mirror. From the auditorium
and from the decor there converge on him the dim
lights of conscious human beings and of the foot-
lights themselves. But the fire with which he burns
is at once that of his inner passion and of that focal
point at which he stands. He lights up in each
member of his audience an accomplice flame.
—André Bazin, (tr.) H. Gray,
'Theatre & Cinema' (1951 / 2005)

At a local bookstore a few days ago, I found TALES OF THE BARK LODGES (1919), by Bertrand N.O. Walker (birth name of Hen-Toh). It's a collection of the stories he remembers being told as a child, published in an attempt to preserve the heritage of the Wyandot people. Walker describes storytelling equal parts entertainment, as instruction, but I really bought it for the compelling detail ending his introduction: it was only during Winter that the people would risk telling these stories, understanding that the spirits of nature were asleep at that time. To tell the stories at another time of year would risk their overhearing so much being said about them, risk offending them.

Another thing I wanted to pick up on that you said, was about the in-between moments. Bazin said that cinema happens between frames. That's where film is really located for the audience. We might say that SCHNEEWITTCHEN is two thirds comprised of those in-between parts, stretched, naked and unspooled as it is. It isn't that there is no image. It is that the aspect of the film that is experienced, and not usually seen, is exposed, reflective.

I mentioned earlier the gaze...

[...]

Playing on the tension between film as controlling the dimension of time (editing, narrative) and film as controlling the dimension of space (changes in distance, editing), cinematic codes create a gaze, a world, and an object, thereby producing an illusion cut to the measure of desire. It is these cinematic codes and their relationship to formative external structures that must be broken down before mainstream film and the pleasure it provides can be challenged.
—Laura Mulvey, 'Visual Pleasure in Narrative Cinema' (1975)

EVANS

What is the etymology of the word gaze? The male gaze, in a gendered way, is the primary focus of Mulvey's attention. It looks like its Scandinavian origin—*to stare, look steadily and intently*—is somehow related to the old Norse—*to heed something of power*. To heed means to take notice of something, to do something. But to take heed is slightly different, more formal. If you heed something—TAKE HEED in the Shakespearean sense—it's not just looking at that 'something,' even observing it attentively. To heed is suggestive, almost like fate or fortune is involved... There're larger forces at work if you don't heed it; bad things could happen to you. That seems to me quite striking in relation to the idea of storytelling; of the fire and darkness we'd already mentioned. Not least the fact that the fairy tale, Grimm's tales, all owe something to a landscape, primarily the Germanic landscape. They were gathering stories in a primarily forestine landscape. The darkness of the forest is a real darkness, you know—populated by wild animals, villains and outlaws and so on—a potent sphere with potential to burn you in different ways. In this sense, this darkness is something significant, you know; there is a genuine need for a story that can lead you through the darkness, quite literally, partly because it sort of distracts you from what's around you, but also because it informs as to the dangers around you.

This seems really important to think about. To gaze, as verb, the gaze, as noun... A gaze represents a fixed and prolonged look; the mind absorbed in that which is looked at. This gaze is the opposite of a guy watching a girl go past on a Paris street, suggestive of something quite fleeting as it is, and an arrogant sort of ownership of that looked-at-object as it passes you and moves away. A gaze is actually way more intense and extended than even Laura's thesis would allow, at least in the kind of concision it seems to suggest.

Here is a great idea: THE GAZEHOUND. GAZE hyphen HOUND. 1560s. An old name for a dog that follows its prey by sight, not scent. A gaze hound is a powerful idea. You know, HERE COMES A GAZE-HOUND.

All those people who left about ten minutes into the first screening of SCHNEEWITTCHEN... They were gazehounds; dogs desperate for sight, you know. To be led by a screen. they receive nothing, because they had to follow all by sound and scent and other senses as yet named.

[...]

When I open my wallet
to show my papers
pay money
or check the time of a train
I look at your face.

The flower's pollen
is older than the mountains
Aravis is young
as mountains go.
 —John Berger, 'And our faces,
 my heart, brief as photos'
 (2014)

It seems interesting that so many of the terminologies that we adopt and accept are taken for granted, and I implicate myself in this completely, you know... Per seeing and sight and attention and looking, you know, WAYS OF SEEING (1972) as John Berger famously put it. Such terms are actually more complex, more blurred and hybrid, than they initially suggest. A gaze is like a sort of psycho-romantic, poetic thing. A much more rigorous looking than, say, staring might be. It's complex.

I think that the removal of an image—concealment of an image and the associative promise of an image—suggests and generates far more perhaps than an image, however brilliant and beautiful and complex, may achieve. It certainly encourages the message of space, which, you know—in your significant telling—is really powerful because, if you go into the cinema for a couple of hours in the afternoon to see something and switch the phone off, you move to initially regard a black screen and more commonly, a flash of images thereafter.

I mean, according to most people's perception, a majoritarian experience, no image is an obstacle. It is the removal of obstacle. That's my experience of it. Everything that you see now, if you watch television, you don't just see as though you're watching something on the screen, you're watching screen on screen on screen on screen.

You know, you're bombarded by images on your phone, but that's now a given. The whole issue of time frame and space... Something we didn't previously consider, but is now a given, it's different. But the black mirror precedes and follows the sequence of images in a darkened space. Here the black mirror informs a black screen, the black leader or so called, which then remains and promises a series of images, but they unfold exclusively within the audience member's mind. It's case by case, individual by individual, as opposed to a collective or connective experience. Whether they share perhaps a collective seeding, you know... There's a lot more going on than any casual dismissal of this as a non-film or even, you know, a non-work because it lacks the fundamental quality that (say, as some critics would have it) of the medium it's chosen to express itself in. To regard SCHNEEWITTCHEN as such is to fundamentally miss the point as regards both what this film is, but also what cinema is, fundamentally. The lineage it comes from, you know, which is not just the image, not just a pedigree of image technologies and photography through to, you know, now—wherever we're going with holograms, et cetera, and art... Actually, you know, storytelling is as much an audio prompt as it is anything like a visual cue. It's that storytelling that goes all the way back. The flicker of the fire on the wall and all of those things. The idea of differing thicknesses of darkness, one of which might be a creature moving towards you, you know, from between the trees.

[...]

32		The Unfree Man
A		He stands and harks: what does he hear?
		What sound is ringing in his ear?
		What struck him down? What mortal fear?
B		Who once wore chains, will always think
		That he is followed by their clink.

—Friedrich Nietzsche, (tr.) W. Kaufmann, 'Scherz, List und Roche' / Joke, Cunning, & Revenge,' *Die Fröhliche Wissenschaft* / *The Gay Science* (1887 / 1974)

SCHTINTER

It is unusual for a film to be so occupied by language. Like the flood narrative, most cultures and religions who've made marks to communicate tell a story about the consequence of its creation (in losing memory and so losing ourselves). In Greek mythology, Hermes—the messenger God—shows his father what he has done, 'Look, dad, now people will never forget!' And Zeus responds by saying 'Au contraire, son, now people really will forget.' With writing we needn't remember, but if we don't remember we lose the map of ourselves; if we don't know where we came from, it's very hard to know where we're going. Maybe it doesn't matter. I still believe the old cliche of it being in the going, and never in the destination, though all the propaganda now is fixed on arrival. The toys that we are provided with today are designed to support this, to contract out the function of memory, as it relates to criticality. You don't need to remember, and as that old cliche goes...

EVANS

No, you don't need to remember. And it's also about, you know, the connection between writing as a form of recording and film. They're distinct forms, but one grows out of the other. Obviously, there is an argument that, the more you have to write, the more you can forget. You outsource memory to the page. Now, we outsource all this memory of both our own lives and a wider knowledge of the world to phones, to other platforms. So, absolutely, there is a journey that begins with writing, which—of course—the practice of oral storytelling around the fire absolutely challenges. And there's no doubt that when you do have a culture which is primarily oral and non-pathographic, memory is passed down very differently. It's configured and analysed and stored and passed on in extremely different ways. Consider Inuit culture, Northern Canadian Inuit cultures. They effectively moved from an oral Indigenous tradition to video diaries in one generation; from the spoken to—at that juncture, you know—the most hyper-visual, most modern form, and just before the Internet came to call.

Zacharias Kunuk, you know? I mean, literally a single generation. Kunuk, and his feature film, ATANARJUAT (which won a major prize at Cannes in 2001); the first feature film to be written, directed and acted entirely in the Inuktitut language, retelling an Inuit legend passed down through centuries of oral tradition... There you've literally got the elision. An incredible elision. Thousands of years, in a second, passing onto something else; something moving from the spoken to the visual, not to the written. We didn't write a novel, and we might have written a book, but that's not the point.

So, and in terms of what we've been speaking about as regards the sort of message space of the auditorium, it is a really significant choice to solely make one print of the film on 35mm, and to make that the only means by which it might be seen, I mean exclusively. More often than not, you'll be travelling with the print. It's a live presentation as much as it is single, one-off event screening. Could you think a little bit more for us about those choices? What it means in relation to the message space for you? Obviously, in media terms, you are directly challenging the digital saturation of our moment, but also—on another level (and I mean, this is obviously a kind of devil's advocate kind of question)—you're directly reducing the possibility of circulation, as regards the message space that you control and then choose to show within.

SCHTINTER

Digital is the reproduction of dawn at Stonehenge. A digital signal is flat, it is numerical. However magnificent, it is a flat representation of the seen. A dead representation of living matter. The analogue signal, meanwhile, is waves; it is living matter, and it moves as living matter moves. It flickers, as the fire flickers. It captures, the ghosts dance. And you needn't be an aficionado, or a snob, to recognise that. The audience feels it, I am sure, and—being a physical artwork—we want that experience to be replicated as imminently as possible for as many people as possible, and to show the work in the way it was conceived: as a print, for the space it was meant to be shown in: the cinema. If it was shot on film, it ought to be shown on film. At the same time, it is practical. This is an independent production the independence of which any independent production would find unrecognisable. The print's funding has been pawned from various other sources, and it's an expensive business. We have but means for one, as much as I'd like to see dozens moving around the world at the same time. The advantage of this is that it becomes, I hope, a significant event, something that people actually have to travel to, and depending at what point in its journey you see it: it will be a different film. Physical matter bears its scars. I'm excited by that aspect of it, the print's signs of simple use: the grind of the teeth of the projector; the gate through which the matter passes.

> [...]
> Baby, take a good look at my face
> Oh, you'll see my smile looks out of place
> Yeah, just look closer, it's easy to trace
> The tracks of my tears
> —Marvin Tarplin / Warren Moore / William Jr. Robinson, as performed by Smoky Robinson, 'The Tracks of My Tears' (1965)

See IN PRAISE OF SHADOWS, wherein Junichiro Tanizaki writes about the cardinal sin of polishing brassware. Its value and its beauty, he describes, in Japanese culture at that time (in 1933, reflecting on the recent past), is in its signs of use, that is of life.

> [...]
> As a general matter we find it hard to be really at home with things that shine and glitter. The Westerner uses silver and steel and nickel tableware,

and polishes it to a fine brilliance, but we object to
the practice. While we do sometimes indeed use silver
for teakettles, decanters, or saké cups, we prefer not
to polish it. On the contrary, we begin to enjoy it only
when the lustre has worn off, when it has begun to
take on a dark, smoky patina. Almost every house-
holder has had to scold an insensitive maid who has
polished away the tarnish so patiently waited for.
—Junichirō Tanizaki, (tr.) T.J. Harper
& E.G. Seidensticker, *In Praise of Shadows*
(1933 / 1977)

Life is located in the event. The chosen presentation format is a gesture in defence of the event, of coming together and watching together, and an insistence on protecting the architectures—the people's palaces—designed for this.

I think it's also important to point out that all of this is possible, not because we have a big budget, but because we don't have a budget at all. You, Gareth, aren't some grisly producer intent on making back their investment in the film, because you haven't invested in it anything but time and care. In making this point, it's a careful balancing act between keeping the enchantment and the impossibility of this project intact, not peeling back the curtain too much, while also communicating to people, encouraging people, that it is possible to make what you want to make without the interference and compromise most would presume part and parcel. Anything of any worth can be made for next to nothing. This is not a justification for artists not being paid, not at all, but if you think you can't deliver on your vision without several million pounds, or even just the right kind of oil paint, something has gone very wrong, and—with few exceptions—can only get worse.

EVANS

There're a few things to pick up on here.

Obviously, there's a practical, financial underpinning to the single print realisation, but it actually becomes inevitable, and we've expressed very well as to why. Not least, because then there is that singular experience of acumen, as it were—in the print's life, as it travels—and that it may have months on the shelf before it comes out again, and so on and so on. But it will absolutely accumulate its history and it's a singular, unique artifact in that respect. So, it totally fulfils the promise of IN PRAISE OF SHADOWS, the larger Japanese-ultra sort of energies, which I really like. Also, you know, there're degrees of darkness... We've talked about a thickening darkness in storytelling, in the forest. But also, there're degrees of darkness, as regards the form of encounter we'd mentioned earlier, the black leaves of darkness at the end of a projection.

Within the cinema...

In prior preview screenings, we experienced a very dark, Munich auditorium [Filmmuseum München / UnderDox, Munich, 12.10.24]. Outstandingly dark in the best possible way. One's eyes—within the unfolding projection, and very differently so on celluloid—seek out, or heed, darknesses on that very-projective screen. I think this is a really crucial point. I mean, there's the need to see, if one has sight, and project texture into something that supposedly has none, because it can always be found.

The 'absolute black,' so-called—the black that Anish Kapoor saw and failed to copyright (or to own, rather), because he didn't create it, it is beyond creation... Although it might absorb all light, it still exists as a darkness that can be projected onto.

I think there's all sorts of interest in that, you know, conceptually and culturally. The singularity of the print becomes effectively a stand-in for you as an artist as well, right? When, even if you're in the room next to it as it projects—having introduced it and/or speaking after it—the singular artefact is always a kind of avatar of the artist such as, you know, an original manuscript copy of James Joyce's ULYSSES (1922). The single print is trying, not in some kind of idea of art world commodification, to enact itself as the opposite of the reproduced and reproducible mass-market Penguin paperback iteration (something closer to the picture-postcard Stonehenge you'd described). Although it's an empty commodity, it absolutely fulfils the idea of the artefactual. There are all sorts of ruptures and complications that it sets in motion by existing and I think that's why I really like it; the fact that it exists, alongside other extant things, suggests that it can be then placed into a certain kind of economy, not just a financial or a market economy, but also a cultural one. However, for some reason—and which we're trying to sort of get to the bottom of in this conversation, in a way—this work is challenging...

Even though it partly wants to be involved, you know, as a circulating artefact in such economies, it challenges such systems. People get an advance notice of it, or they're approached by one or other of us to show it, and they resist, even though it actually completely fits into these circulatory economies, on one level. It might be a more left-field version of an artefact, but it's still an artefact, still to be shown, and it's not going to be shown again and again and again… They can choose to show it once, these cinemas. In fact, in most cases, that's all we're asking them to do. You know, it's a seventy-minute work, it's absolutely at the shorter end of things. And yet, as you said rightly, there is a huge pressure on conventional cinema exhibits, not least obviously to show a contracted title in all available slots, but they literally cannot take these works off programme without financial penalty and thereby conceivably limit possibilities, as regards a relationship with a studio or distributor, and in terms of future titles. So, they literally can't screen it, and won't screen it, unless they feel extremely confident about their own audience space, their own programming viability. In this regard, again, this work is revealing… Revealing something without necessarily attending to the fallacies and monopolies inherent to industrial film culture, something outside and beyond the responsibilities or limitations of individual programmers and venues, I think. It's very interesting, because it seems to me that, as you say, if it was framed—and let's use the word 'packaged' —as a kind of singular piece of event cinema, with potentially some cosplay going on around SNOW WHITE… The idea that people will read the fairytale before and after as generally configured in various ways, then this work could do far, far better than the vast majority of almost empty, week-based screenings of any big, so-called temporal release. It really does present a literal challenge, you know, to the very core of what the cinematic experience is. And this is all before you even enter the room.

    There are very few works like this; I mean, ever fewer as the years go on, in the sense of a feature-length work that has the possibility (in terms of its production and/or the involvement of certain talents and so on) to actually reach an audience. It's really a fascinating idea and articulation of something that—and I think I'm safe in saying, was not at the heart of the project's intentions—has actually revealed itself to exactly be such a work.

    There's also the fact of time involved, because SCHNEE-WITTCHEN is, by measure, a short film—a short feature—and yet, it seems to be threatening time, as we've experienced it by way of some audiences, but more primarily from the structures of industry, the film industry, and the venues and festivals. They are literally threatened by its duration in this way. If it was a sort of eight or twelve-minute short, I imagine it would show reasonably easily, and relatively swiftly, in various short film festivals around the world. But it's a feature, and so suddenly it claims a space that they are literally not prepared to allow—geographically, in terms of the auditorium—but also temporarily, in terms of its duration. I think it's as though what appears to be quite a discreet and intimate and modest undertaking—to tell Robert Walser's adaptation of SNOW WHITE by various means—cinematically has suddenly become, without us intending it, and not really pushing it, something more argumentative.

Theoretically, we're not conceptualising the work out of existence, we're just talking about what it is and how it moves in the world. It suddenly has become this kind of dangerous force, not just to the forces of commodification and the market, but dangerous always to the idea of what cinema itself is.

It reminds me, in the darkness of its rectangle... It reminds me of Santiago Sierra, the Anarchist artist, and his 'Black Flag,' the black flag of Anarchist tradition, but when he installed it at the North and South Poles it becomes something extremely threatening to people. A black flag on the whiteness of the poles; it speaks to the ways in which (and extent to which) they are rapidly disappearing.

In a way, what Sierra is doing is both challenging the idea of any kind of territorial, national, nation-state ownership of land areas and territories that absolutely do not deserve to be claimed in such a way, but also—and crucially—that flag represents a force of upset, of subversion, an inversion of the expected order by forces that are outside of control, which is exactly what SCHNEEWITTCHEN is doing as an artwork, as just mentioned, in its own territories. That Sierra's is a black flag on a white landscape suggests also—and again I won't push this idea further than merely mentioning it—other forms of hierarchy and dominance, shall we say, of landscapes and peoples and cultures and histories. I'm not claiming that Sierra has set out to directly confront such ideas—to explore, with his marking, such conceptual and tangible territories—but in that respect, we make these associations... They all join together in a challenge to established hierarchical structures, these territories of thinking—whether a periodisation or colonisation or patriarchy—or whatever which way it is directed, they're all ideas concerning a certain way of being in the world. Things like this—both flag and film—fundamentally challenge our complacencies, without ever setting out or claiming to do so, but they just do. They accumulate association and a kind of grit as they make their way in the world, and I think that's really interesting.

SCHTINTER

Black is the only colour with every other colour in it. Paradoxically, the black of our material film can never project black. Reliant on light, there is no such thing. 'Black light' is a marketing term for UV; invisible to humans. And I might add that the 'black screen' in relation to SCHNEEWITTCHEN, as with BRANCA DE NEVE, is actually a presumption made by the viewer. And it's interesting you bring up Santiago Sierra's flag, an incredible project and image—that pole-mounted black fabric in the open field of pure white snow, at the south pole—because how can it be that a blank piece of fabric, in an 'empty' place or a crowded one, causes such disdain and fear? All of the other flags, except perhaps ISIS, fly without much notice, and even with support. All flags are preposterous! And that's what I take from the black flag of Anarchism. They're impressive, they often look good at the top of buildings, massive pieces of fabric moved by the wind, but whatever your political stripe to make a coherent case for them? Come off it. I think the pushback to Sierra's anti-occupation through the flag is a subliminal acknowledgement of this (preposterousness) by its critics.

That Anarchism has lost its way in the popular imagination is curious. The merchandised pop song; the cushy academic post from which to espouse its virtues? Or just another victim of Silicon Death Valley... These things don't exactly enhance its legitimacy, or potency, as an approach, and it was never deserving of its 'ism,' but as a global conversation turns to the re-localisation of small communities, and the relative autonomy that implies... it's curious.

I think people forget how young the United States is as a country, and how long warring factions—namely, Capitalists and Anarchists—fought for its future. 23 Wall Street still bears the bullet holes and the shrapnel marks from the deadliest attack in US history until 9/11, which was ostensibly an Anarchist plot (and the first place I visited when I went to New York City many years ago).

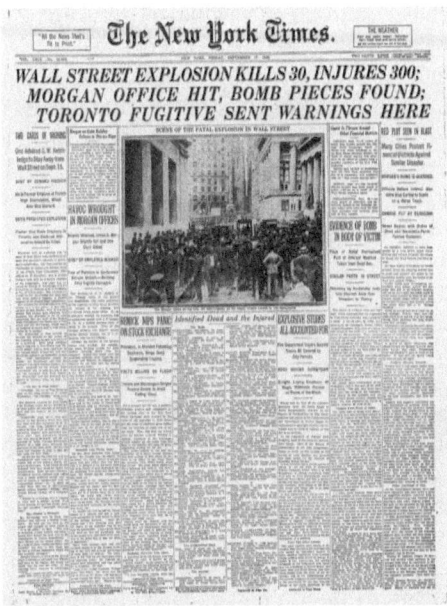
[...]
The New York Times (17 September 1920)

People forget too how recent the invention of the police force is in the UK. Anarchism was, and is, the de facto condition for most people in most places for most of history. Self-government means something very straight forward to me: my freedom, but not at the expense of your freedom. Mutual aid is necessary. Between ordinary people, really much more recently than most people would think—in an English village, for example—the situation you'd have witnessed was something like Anarchy: I have something you need, you have something I need. We trade. We must get along. It's harder not to get along. What breaks that is the mental illness of greed backed up by the capacity of ultra-violence, and the wielding of the magic wand that says, 'Thus, this actually belongs to me.' The village I grew up in took its name from what would have been called an Anarchist uprising if it had happened later in history. A wealthy landowner exorbitantly raised the toll to cross the gates in that part of the road, and these were burned down (by a forebear, so the legend goes). The emblem of the local cricket club is gates on fire. Weirdly, I only recently recognised the hellish connotations — appropriate for the majority of the characters who inhabit the place.

All evidence says that the current setup is untenable—an economy that only flows outwards doesn't work. Cryptocurrency has often grappled with this, and though obviously not expressly 'Anarchist,' there's the Lewes pound, which is tethered to the British pound but exists to ensure money spent locally stays local, inspired as it was by Massachusetts' BerkShares tethered to the US dollar. In Iran, the mosques have free energy, so bitcoin miners moved all of their servers into the house of God, a practical prayer to dig with.

EVANS

That's interesting, although it's propagandising as well, but it's very confused politically...

I find it very interesting that it seems now in America there's this moment where people have—and it's so strange that they should be voting for a Republican to achieve this—but the American people have reflected on an imperial project lasting well over a century, in which many of the flag-flying interventions they've made, they have lost, and now they have voted resoundingly for an end to that. I do not think that Donald Trump represents this position, but that's not the point. I think that it's interesting. It's interesting because when we're talking about these [cultural] institutions, we're talking about programming, we're talking about the targeting of a particular kind of person, their remit... They do not consider the kind of person living in North America's rural geographies. (Well, they don't because we're probably talking about English cinemas here.) But what I mean to say is that someone in a rural part of America who has perhaps lost their son or daughter is experiencing the consequence of a flag-flying war in a place that has absolutely nothing to do with them. Sierra's use of colour, black being the only colour that contains all, is perfect because the threat to America is the fact that—if it was understood and acted on by all people, as represented here by all colours as it were, all kinds of people —then that would be the ultimate threat to the state, however configured on a higher art scale.

What you'd said about mysticism in interesting. Anarchism is a political philosophy, and therefore it's an *-ism* and there is obviously a collective loss in *-isms*, of belief in *-isms* now, from the beginnings of the 20th century and on. An iota of that loss of belief is for understandable reasons and—in other cases—it is because one *-ism* prevailed, and that's Capitalism. It exists, particularly under its neoliberal moniker, more acutely than anything else, and all other *-isms* have had to dissimulate in a kind of Darwinian survivalist business. So, Anarchism can't exist, but you're right in saying that it's the fusion with Anarchism and statehood in the popular imagination and Anarchy as a state of negative conflictual disorder that has been a central propaganda position whenever any kind of group of people threatens some kind of disorder against the state and its structures.

And yes, Anarchism has an adjectival power that exists outside of a purely political or philosophical space. I don't think I've ever heard anyone be accused on the street. in some kind of altercation, 'You're a real Socialist, you really are a Socialist... There was massive Socialist behaviour in the centre of Hereford on Saturday night.'

SCHTINTER

You say that, but the right in America calls everyone a Communist, or 'left,' as a slur.

EVANS

No, they do, that's true. This really, really confuses me; they talk about the left in the broadest sense, and I mean Anarchism and Communism... There're overlaps, sure. Maybe an Anarchist would prefer more to be in a room with a Communist than they would a Capitalist but—state / no state—you know, they are diametrically opposed positions. I think contemporary Anarchism needs to move its target; not just in terms of questions of statehood, but as the state is now a manifestation of corporate and military forces, and so on... I mean, the point about being a Communist doesn't work here in the same way, you know; in the UK, it's the default, comic setting, as opposed to the oppositional slur in America. But I think the allegation of 'Anarchist,' the Anarchist idea and its colouration, shall we say—with the black flag in mind—really serves SCHNEEWITTCHEN and its purposes very productively. There's the 'Black Square,' Malevich's 'Black Square' of 1915—his [sic] portrait of his own 'desperate struggle to free art from the ballast of the objective world' configured for the canvas and framed in a gallery context. The work sort of unsettled that space, the white cube of the gallery, kicking off a new tradition. We have the same parallel going on here as we do with Sierra's flag placed at the poles. You know, Malevich's 'Black Square' arguably contains—if you take your very valid point to its conclusion—all other paintings, just as Sierra's flag contains all flags. And so... It's so fascinating.

SCHTINTER

And the pupil of the eye... The blackest ever black is the pupil of the eye.

[...]
Black is the colour of my true love's hair,
Her lips are something rosy fair.
The prettiest face and the daintiest hands,
I love the grass whereon she stands.
—TRADITIONAL / see George Crumb,
Unto the Hills: American Songbook III
(2002)

EVANS

Absolutely. And, you know, so, if you take that logic and you apply the nature of the black rectangle, or the square—containing all of its previous incarnations and all its possible incarnations

—then it becomes such an acute project. It's what appears to be a reduction to essences, in terms of the so-called absence or removal of an image but actually, as you'd yourself said earlier, is the opposite. It's a profligate sewing of all images, or in this case—all films—within its border. I think that's a far more productive way to think about it, you know. The black. Both for us to think about and for programmers who are accepting the film into their programme... To talk about it in relation to their audiences.

[...]

I recall one particular sunset. It lent an ember to my bicycle bell. Overhead, above the black music of telegraph wires, a number of long, dark-violet clouds lined with flamingo pink hung motionless in a fan-shaped arrangement; the whole thing was like some prodigious ovation in terms of colour and form! It was dying, however, and everything else was darkening, too; but just above the horizon, in a lucid, turquoise space, beneath a black stratus, the eye found a vista that only a fool could mistake for the spare parts of this or any other sunset. It occupied a very small sector of the enormous sky and had the peculiar neatness of something seen through the wrong end of a telescope. There it lay in wait, a family of serene clouds in miniature, an accumulation of brilliant convolutions, anachronistic in their creaminess and extremely remote; remote but perfect in every detail; fantastically reduced but faultlessly shaped; my marvellous tomorrow ready to be delivered to me.
—Vladimir Nabokov, *Speak, Memory* (1951)

It's not that people are getting less for their ticket price, they're getting everything, you know? If they think of it like that, then what they're actually being asked to transact around is not really the film itself, not at all. You know, the final, final analysis —after all other levels of encounter have been considered—is actually a transaction with their own imagination.

How limited or limitless is that?

That seems to me to be the bottom line of the whole project, really. It's about imagination and image and how rich an image-nation may be. That's what imagination is, almost literally; it's a territory. A country of image. How populated is that country? Their country?

Of course, you want to take that further—a little bit further, philosophically—and then you need to talk about the interior landscape of one's own reality and the external panorama… Many, many people have observed that we create an external reality from the interior landscape, which, you know—as has been articulated so well—is the real, and the external world a projection.

So, all of these ideas—all these theoretical and philosophical, conceptual, cultural, artistic ideas, and even psychological and psychoanalytic positions—are concepts within the film.

I'm not expecting someone to get all that—as they come out and have a beer following the screening—as it has taken me quite a long time to realise such, and our conversations have been crucial to that process, you know? But once one starts thinking about it, these associations just start to multiply. They're not forced, you know? I'm not struggling to think of something to say here. It's just that once you start to follow a certain line that is not the expected one—and refuses the staple frameworks of argument that are usually imposed on a work like this—then you've a considerably more fertile space. You certainly won't be having a conversation like this, you know, when you leave PADDINGTON IN PERU. I mean, you may have some quite rich conversations around border control; migration; North and South; imperial and colonial histories, et cetera…

SCHTINTER

There is a gasp of liberating potential in PADDINGTON IN PERU, even if the bear has otherwise been victim to the tyranny of franchise. What I mean is, spoiler alert: El Dorado is revealed to Paddington, but rather than it being a city filled with gold, it's full of oranges. Perfect oranges. The oranges are the gold. The kids are being told that that gold material doesn't mean much. Riches really are communities formed around trees bearing fruit. Refreshment is everything, and Vitamin C, and owning the means of production. Thereafter, the film really loses it way. Paddington industrialises the perfect orange grove, putting the freedom-loving community to work in the production of marmalade.

The issue is, and this is a real oversight and betrayal by the well-meaning maker. He systematises the grove, growling 'more sugar, more sugar,' which is poison. Like, to a lesser degree, tomatoes are poison until they're cooked, and milk is poison until it's turned into cheese. Orson Welles said that it's irrelevant where you come from. It's where you choose to die. And Paddington, unbelievably—yearlong sunshine, all naked bears, endless marmalade made with God's own oranges—heads back to West London. I haven't been so bored watching a film for a long time, in spite of the revelation of soft oranges where hard gold was always believed to be. This perhaps goes back to the contemplation implicit in gaze, and the generative state of boredom. Contemplation and boredom, I think, are only a whisker away from one another. If boredom is denied us is contemplation too?

EVANS

Yes, completely. I mean, you know, I genuinely—and this might sound ridiculous, and I'm not claiming any special abilities here—but, as an adult I'm not really ever bored. I don't know why I would say that that's different from being a child, although —as a child—I'm sure I was, because I didn't necessarily have the available tool kit to think about things in a different way then, but I'm never bored really, and I haven't been bored for probably my whole adult life. There's always something, you know? Whether you're stuck in a waiting room and there's no reading material—and this is before phones—or anywhere where there's not a source of stimulation provided in the form of some kind of artefact, whether it be a book or a film or a notebook or whatever. Something that demands attention, demands the ability of people to watch it. I'm speaking of public spaces, an airport or such like. But you can always start spinning stories to yourself.

I'm not particularly claiming that I'm a great person because of that, I just do not find there to be an absence of stimulation in almost any environment. You can always make these associative journeys, as we've been sort of doing in the course of this conversation, I think.

Anything can prompt that journeying. You know, there's a great poem, and I've tried to find it—I'm reading now through his collection—and partly to try and find it because I've searched, and I can't remember it. George Oppen. The Imagist (well, he started as an Imagist). The very committed Communist

American poet, George Oppen. In the poem, he talks about looking at a wall, you know—staring at a wall—but the wall is made up of unique bricks, they're bricks of the old world and not the industrial monoculture of today. Every brick has a story, every brick is clay, you know—coming from a different part of the clay fields—and they've all weathered in different ways. Moss and cracks and such-like.

> [...]
>
> So small a picture,
> A spot of light on the curb, it cannot demean us
>
> I too am in love down there with the streets
> And the square slabs of pavement—
> —George Oppen, 'Of Being Numerous /
> Sections 1–22'
> (1968)

He's going back to what you were saying about Japanese culture, you know? He says that this wall—and not in any way that closes down the experience; it's an opening, rather; a massive opening—becomes a screen. Not one that conceals reality, but actually one that—like cinema—opens reality up to its almost infinite possibility. And I do feel like that. I really feel like that almost all the time in the sense that you can walk around and, as long as you are still conscious, then you can actually get something from almost any scenario.

Now, I don't want to claim that I have been properly tested—you know, with an endless duration and the lack of external stimuli—of course not. That would be a different story. But in terms of how we talk about boredom on a daily basis in a stable society... I think it needs to be challenged regularly and absolutely. And the content of this flipside to boredom doesn't require special training or anything, no special skill, it just requires one to be open to a kind of associative tangential possibility.

SCHTINTER
And to go. To go, to go, to go out into the world.
(I am grateful that my parents would, as far as I can remember, affectionately tell me to get lost. Be back by teatime.)

Absolutely. Completely. I think that's what—in a way—what the film offers, you know? Our cast—I don't want to speak on behalf of them at all—but I think our cast were taken when they were presented with this project, and they'd all articulated a rationale differently to themselves, as to why they wanted to do it. But clearly, they were all—they all are—very committed people, committed to the project—and let's say the great cultural project —which is curiosity.

They're all curious about what art forms they work within are capable of, what they can do, what they can hold, rather than just completely repeating the same thing every time, however brilliant and dumb. You know, Toby has spoken explicitly about this... What he looks for when he's presented with scripts and roles, and so on. And I'm sure there's no difference in essence, in that case, as regards Julie or Stacy or Stephen or Hanns, you know. Whatever project they're presented with, they'll be looking to do something they haven't done before and it refracts their own abilities through its lens.

I think that's absolutely the case here, you know. This project asks them to do something else; it's a production explicitly based around very different ways of doing things, but even as the lowest level industrial project. Crucially—and this is very important to its success, I think—it blurs art forms, both in its own expression and its making. It fuses what some people would call radio drama, let's say, with the stage; obviously with regards to storytelling, with writing, with moving image work; and with the idea of the still image, with photography. It is a different kind of project. Gesamtkunstwerke—which we've touched on earlier, by other means—in that it contains all artworks within it, and great sound design and scoring. It's a project that tries to kind of contain the world, or at least not to contain, but to propose the world.

For most people's purposes, this proposition stems from removal; in what the project removes an element from its artistic palette, while simultaneously proposing the widest possible vision.

It proposes a world as opposed to framing a world of almost infinite possibilities simply by removing one element —a characteristic that people more commonly associate with music, say—and by removing an element that people would describe as the idea of the image. It proposes the largest possible visual palette, which is your own imagination. I think that that point about the imagination is really key.

And another thing I'd say, the last point I wanted to make, regards the idea of time.

Just one more thought about time.

It seems to me that the duration of this film is significant in the culture, and for all the reasons we've described. It challenges the awkward tumult and omnidirectional character of the mainstream, regardless of how it works. The time it proposes within itself, it expands, because of this idea of the so-called removal. Once you remove a reference from the visual prompt, you enter a very different kind of durational space, particularly in the dark—in the auditorium—where the screen itself has a different texture of darkness. We cannot separate the time and place of showing from the time and place within the film itself, which is absolutely really crucial. We know the dimensions of the frame and the dimensions of the screen, depending on the cinema, but it's the imaginative space— that of the narrative unfolding—that pictures a landscape that every single person will configure and sketch differently. That's the crucial point. In that way, it's one of the great provocative artworks; it does all this without declaration. That's so important. It doesn't say, I am now going to subvert contemporary culture by doing x and y and z. It's absolutely a self-reflexive artwork. It's fully aware of its own medium, the limitations and possibilities.

SCHNEEWITTCHEN is not proposing, rhetorically, any of the ideas that we've talked about here. It contains them, but they're buried within its genetic coding, if you like, within its DNA. And that's why I think it stands and is much more rigorous and creatively and conceptually provocative and rewarding than anything that would declare such concepts on anything like the surface of its expression.

And that's the crucial aspect of most regular work. You know, it forces you up against the limit—which is the limit of its own creative possibility—because it's not trying to do anything else except more or less successfully tell a story in whichever way. I think that's where SCHNEEWITTCHEN's real strength lies. It all comes back to this idea of tension between presence and absence.

Of course, both of them contain the other—presence and absence—and logically are evidence of the other.

When someone is removed from a picture, they become far more present to us than... I don't have just an individual photograph in mind, I mean, removed from our world. They become very much more present to us. It ties in with the idea of the ways in which we don't see monuments until they're taken down. It is then that we see them. Its removal draws attention to itself in ways that are both creative and productive, but also obviously irritate many, many people. And why is that? Why is someone irritated by that? That's the real question. Why are they irritated by a prompt to reflection of thought? In a sonic way, that reminds me of what Jung said about noise. He said, you know, people will seek some kind of sound in their space, whatever their space is, to avoid the silence of the interior, and which people are then forced to confront. That impulse is absolutely at work here, which is why we see people leave.

SCHTINTER

In response to what you're describing about the threat of the film, it feels important to consider Monteiro's film, and what inspired such anger and resentment in people and critics at the time of its making. To my mind, with the film that he made, and in the way he made it, he was referencing what I've described about censorship and intervention, by the individuals and institutions who have the cash. The anger was justified, they said, by the production's use of public money. They were basically arguing that there wasn't enough to see, to justify the use of the money in its making.

I wanted to know if, all of these years later, it was possible to tell the same joke twice; in that way, this is a homage to Monteiro's sense of humour and mischief—and it seems that, yes, it is possible (to tell the same joke). It'll be up to the audience to decide whether the joke is eventually on us, considering that neither public nor private funds availed. In any case, the second time around, people are potentially even more upset by it. And yet, as you've said, the only real investment is one of people's time and enthusiasm.

EVANS

Exactly. The contentious element of it in its using public subsidies has disappeared entirely. Even as an absolutely private project—obviously, made with less than nothing as it was—it is perhaps even more frustrating for people because it's pulled itself out of the transactional exchange. We're led to believe that our reason for making something is to afford us a certain kind of sustenance that has an entirely material and immediate expression in the world, rather than the poetics of the imagination.

SCHTINTER

I know plenty of 'makers' who won't move until they're granted the money to produce the thing. I understand this as practical, as much as it is tactical. The culture is suspicious of that which is self-funded, as though it's somehow necessary to self-fund, or worth less. Our mutual friend Louis Benassi often wasn't taken seriously, in part for funding his own work, but for him the hard and unrelenting labour that paid badly would only be justified, beyond a roof over the table with food on it, by an investment in his practice. Ben Morea, the painter who is probably best known for his activities with UP AGAINST THE WALL MOTHERFUCKERS, ended up painting because he felt that it was the practice he could find that was closest to being able to do something for nothing. As we've already discussed: less investment with less interest means less risk of you being manipulated and conforming and essentially reproducing the propaganda that keeps you and those around you repeating the same shit. This is a hard path to follow, and I don't personally suffer for it in the same way (largely by working exceptionally hard in lots of different fields to afford myself a precarious but consistent measure of luxury). Increasingly, I do think that almost any action is justifiable if it can break the bind of the mind forg'd manacles.

EVANS

Indeed. The crucial thing is that the position sought by Louis or Morea—whomever we want to think about—is that it goes back to the idea of self-publishing. Publishing in paper and print terms.

The idea is a simple one: that no one else will endorse or validate your work, and therefore you have to do it yourself. There is an urgent small press scene now—a massive expansion in zine production—where people are self-producing in all sorts of ways. Effectively, you know—and certainly as regards print—for no money whatsoever. These projects just pay for themselves. Just one copy in the library... That tradition is absolutely one we would sign up to, although it seems that the institutional world has decided such works are not worth recognising; are not even especially knowledgeable. Nonetheless, we now have the wider culture and are just doing it.

The irony is that there've been so many waves of zine culture from, you know, that we've works that then become valuable at auction, but that's not their fault. They obviously aren't making the work with that intention in mind, the small, calculating number... But the crucial idea that by self-making and therefore by the self-supporting, self-financing, self-producing, self-gathering of the materials, et cetera, you're somehow not as valid as we are? It's the greatest lie and argument used by industrial, corporatised and commodified Capitalist culture, whatever you want to call it. It stands against individual activity and autonomous realisation, which again comes back to Anarchism, doesn't it?

SCHTINTER

Yes, and disbelief and the will to damage or bury the work by those who cannot stand that you've done it without towing the party line, without acknowledging the firmly established social and financial hierarchies. When it's apparent they can't destroy it, instead they attempt to possess some part of it, as a relative truth in service of their total lie.

EVANS

You know, our labour in exchange is different from that of finance or goods cultures—and obviously, the temporal concerns that mean that we can't be doing something else while we're doing that—we can't be contributing to the system and or in whatever small way benefiting from it. It's a double rejection of that temporal theft by the system—of our time in labour terms and in terms of refusing to pay—to pay for that time ourselves when we're making it. I think that's really important.

It comes back finally to the gift of the cast, the gift the cast gave to the project. They gave their time to a project which they could not necessarily secure in advance any guaranteed outcome from, and which they basically signed up to for Equity's lowest-level rate. But more importantly, they signed up on the basis of trust, and that's the crucial element.

Without trust, there is no viable, functioning humane society. SCHNEEWITTCHEN speaks to a certain kind of truth in making and the truth of possibility; of what culture is and can be, or has been, now and into the future: a space of possibility to remake and reinvent.

But it doesn't play with the idea that questions need be answered. It asks a question by itself: what that space is for, and how you find yourself—you, me, everyone who encounters it—within it. This concerns both maker and receiver and audience member alike. It asks such questions at a time when culture itself is being threatened, funding has been withdrawn —whether in the UK or Germany or internationally—and in a scenario whereby culture and freedom of expression are seen as an inherent problem. Books are being taken out of libraries, they're being burnt, et cetera, et cetera, on the left and right and in the centre. You know, we face the threat of expression, the threat to expression, on a daily basis. This is vital, because expression is not the same as overproduction. They're very, very different things. You know, it's not that everyone must and needs and should just constantly produce expression in various, artefactual ways, but the freedom of expression within that is obviously central, unarguable and necessary. However, the point about culturing a threat is inherent within this project and it resists it. SCHNEEWITTCHEN resists that shuttering, arguably removing elements of itself from the ability to be surveilled. It resists the threat to cultural and free expression, and it proposes an alternative that is outside of such forms of control. Increasingly, because it's a project that has based its entire existence on exchanges of trust. The truth it kind of proposes is again outside of qualification and control and surveillance, and the relationship of truth and trust is what makes a viable society one that is liveable into the future. Without those elements in place, on a larger scale, we are in danger of losing what really matters.

Without those elements, then there is no future.

SCHTINTER

Well, that seems like a good place to stop or, if not a place to stop, a place to echo the optimism of Jose Val Del Omar's parallel fairytale end title: SIN FIN, he'd close the credits. Endless.

**SIN FIN /
WITHOUT END**

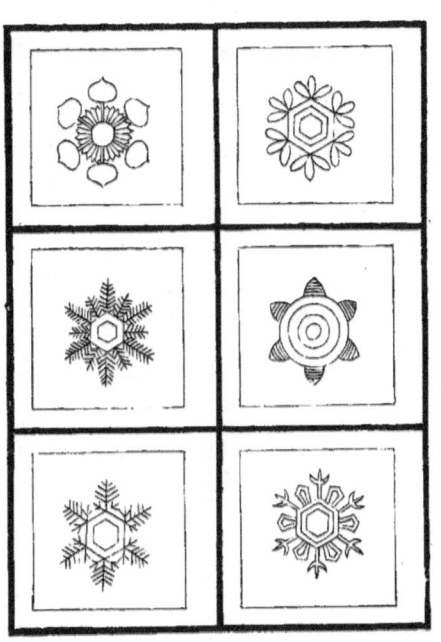

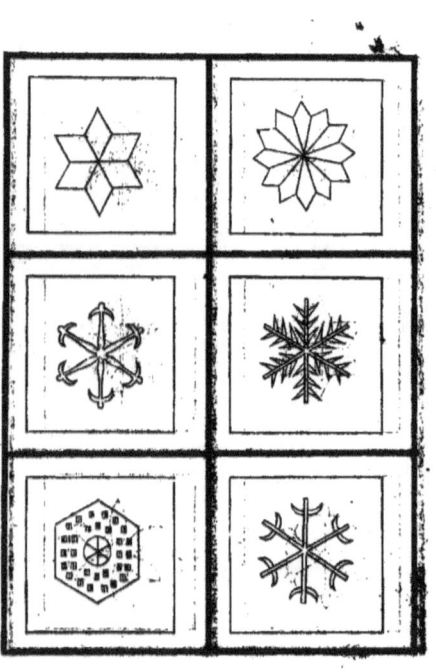

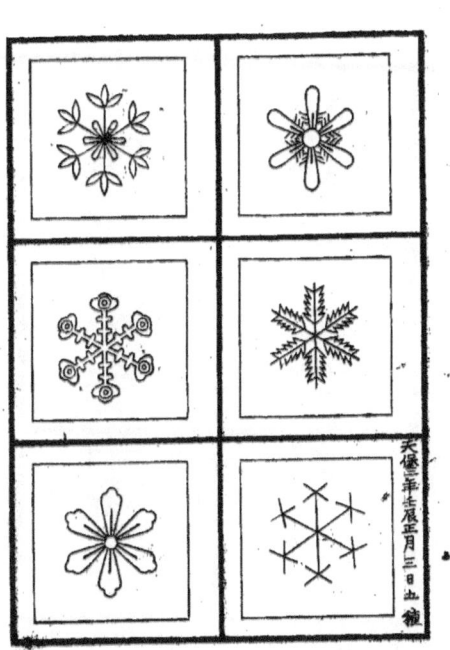

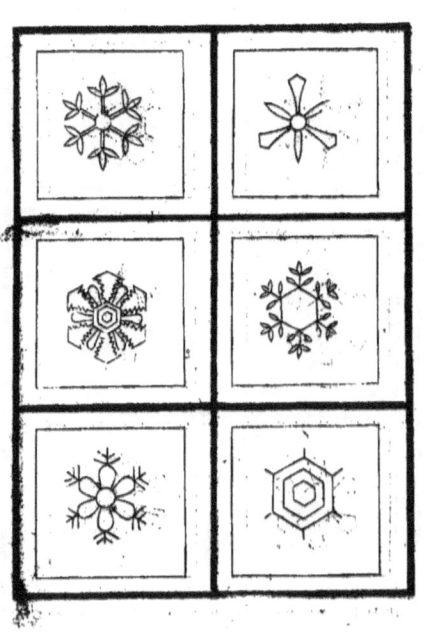

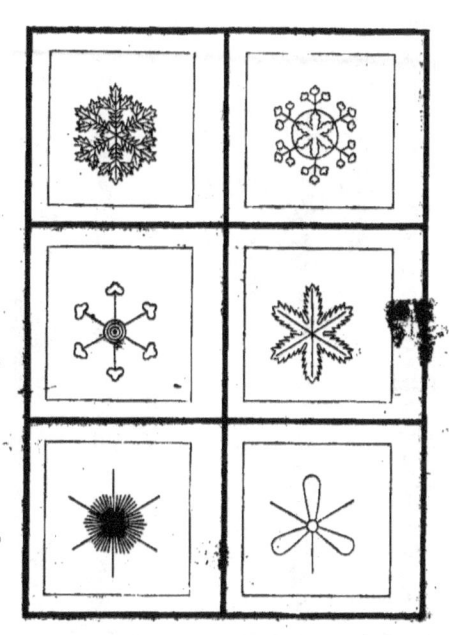

兩間ノ萬物半箇モ眠用無ハ無シ人之ヲ享ルノ人。但ツノ聲色香味ヲ朝美シ却テ真實ノ用ヲ知覺セス人ノ物ニオケル既ニソノ真ヲ知テソノ理ヲ窮メテマタソノ聲色ヲ愛スルトキハ物ソノ究ヲ免レヒ人モ之ニ溺ルヽノ患無シ風花雪月ノ如ク人命ノ係ルトコロ最大ナリシカル二亦茫然省悟セス蓋人情浮華ヲ喜ヒ沈實ヲ疎ム不才國寧當中西ノ諸籍ヲ讀テ粗靈花ノ說ヲ知リソノ功ノ偉ナル

雪華図説 / *Sekka Zusetsu* is a figure collection assembled by Doi Toshitsura, the fourth feudal lord (daimyo) of the Koga Domain, 1832. Koga was located at the centre of the Kantō Plain (central Honshu, the largest desert plain in Japan) and—due to regular, heavy snowfall—its landscape proved an appropriate geography for the amateur observation of snowflakes; termed by Toshitsura as 'snow flowers,' *Sekka*.

Toshitsura began observing snowflakes as a pastime with his own microscope, imported from the Netherlands and, over the course of a twenty-year period, he drew diagrammatic, woodblock studies of these 'flowers'—identifying some ninety-seven unique forms in all—and gathered his research into a self-published volume originally produced for personal remembrance and for his family's records (土井氏 / the Doi clan).

The publication, subsequently, had a great influence on Japanese textile cultures, with snowflake-like patterns (雪華模様) becoming increasingly popular among the Edo population. An original print volume of Toshitsura's work is held in the Printing Museum, Bunkyo-ku, Tokyo, Japan.

*

RECORDED METHOD OF OBSERVATION

1. Put a black cloth outside at night when it seems cold enough to snow.
2. Receive snowflakes upon the cloth.
3. If snowflakes are received, pick them up carefully and relocate them into a black cup.
4. Being careful not to disturb them with your breathe, observe with a microscope.

(*Wikipedia*)

*

OVERSIGHTS
STANLEY SCHTINTER

ON SOUND

I was in Bali for Nyepi some years ago. In the run up to the festival (a ritual casting out of the bad spirits that have accumulated over the course of the year on the island) the entire island stops its normal business. People are either practising the gamelan in the temples or preparing their papier-mâché monsters in the streets. The next day is silence, and to make a sound beyond your four walls means certain arrest. The only sound to rival this one—of the constant din of preparation, and then the explosion of the night, and then the silence—is in Herisau, in the sound of the sane and epic hills traversed by Walser in his final twenty-three years of not writing; of the cowbells advancing and receding. One especially memorable encounter with this space, and its sound was with Bonnetta when we went to take a twenty-three-hour recording at the site Walser fell on Christmas Day. As an aside, we went into the woods by night, up towards Walser's peak, and there we listened to the tired, distant bells and the bats. Bonnetta has a toy that identifies the breed of bat passing by, and night-vision with which to watch them. The audio instrument maps the creature's sound waves and makes audible its night-song. There was an owl too, which—just surpassing the hare in its frequency and proximity—has been a constant in my work, or unwork, beginning or ending: I finished the film in the Rheinland and took a walk out. All of two metres in a clearing in the woodland was an enormous Eurasian Owl that sat, and stared, for minutes, he, she, I.

*

ON THE REMAKE

It was actually A COMÉDIA DE DEUS / GOD'S COMEDY (1996) —my favourite of Monteiro's films—that I wanted to remake, but there was some issue with the rights. As it happens this then becomes more like a homage to Manoel de Oliveira, since he never got to make a film like this one.

*

ON DIRECTION

I need show these actors nothing, but I did present a book. COMET (2019). I knew about Hanns Zischler's other life as poet and academic, familiar with his book and film, KAFKA AT THE MOVIES (1998)—a project that I'd drawn on for LAST MOVIES (2023)—and so I picked up this extraordinary collection of photographs from the Rosetta Space Probe, to which he contributed a brilliant essay. He gets everything in there, from personal reflections of lying in Fiji and witnessing the stars as falling snowflakes and ties it to the starry sky-cloth that architect Karl Friedrich Schinkel designed for THE MAGIC FLUTE in 1816. 'Astral music, a moving picture, standing still.'

The Rosetta probe was the first to land a module on the surface of a comet, and it followed this comet that it took ten years to get to, photographing as it went about harvesting stardust. You see the earth receding into the distance, other planets too, and space, vast and incomprehensible space (that I knowingly foolishly sought to conjure in the film) through which this rock of ice and minerals travels, catching the light, hiding the light. It's unbelievable. And it upended science's understanding of the origin of the solar system. Nobody has even heard of it. And it changed everything. So this is the book, these are the photographs I gave to the cast, and Zischler's essay I privately devoured. 'Think of me,' whispered the dust. The Hale Bopp comet in 1997 I remember as a really significant event, and Zischler describes it as the only comet he's ever seen. That year, 1997—the year that Blake prophesied as the last—did something to my childhood. Ended it, possibly. Diana's death, and what that revealed about the country, and the people around me. Heaven's Gate. And then Gormley's Angel arrives just after Christmas. Mad.

*

SKIES

My grandfather only ever gave me one piece of advice: always look above eye level.

*

TIME

To paraphrase Terence McKenna: which lasts longer, 100 million years where nothing happens, or 10 seconds with 50,000 concurrent events?

Time is only experienced by the events occurring within it. McKenna also talks about the origins of thought and art and magic and so science as a broad tradition in the West, versus the one in the East: we got hung up on matter, and we achieved remarkable things by that hang up: we can light the fire that burns at the heart of the distant star. 'They' were hung up on time: meditating inwards to suspend it; to see what the fuck was going on.

*

ANOTHER ONE ON TIME

The legend goes that the two men who made the Zodiacal clock in St. Mark's Square were officially blinded so that they couldn't make another for anyone else, anywhere else.

*

BLACK
(*Luminous.*)
Colour exists even in total darkness.

*

THE LAST REMAKE
(*Haven't we seen enough?*)
Means the end of something, implying a belief another thing will follow, implies a new story and a new way of storytelling.

*

LITERATURE & CINEMA

(*Probably to pair with Zeus comment, see* p.XLIX.)
Cinema is, like writing, a trap. And a spell.

But whereas writing concerns ideas, cinema concerns ghosts.

*

'Even the seven dwarves are sitting at home by their screens, leaving the pallbearing to random romantics, undaunted volunteers, momentary hopefuls.'
　—Esther Kinsky, (tr.) C. Schmidt,
　WEITER SEHEN / SEEING FURTHER
　(2023 / 2024)*

*

* It is of interest that, per the mercantile 'packaging' of work, in England, Kinsky's SEEING FURTHER would circulate as a 'declaration of love' / in America, as a novel, a work of fiction.

ROBERT WALSER*

First dreamt of becoming an actor.

His protagonists are children, social outcasts, artists, impoverished, marginalised and forgotten.

He was institutionalised for 28 years, his final 23 in Herisau. During these years he did not write, but he walked a lot.

SCHNEEWITTCHEN was his first published work, probably written in Munich (1901) and published in the Rheinland in a publication that sought to lean arts focus away from Berlin and onto this region.

From the asylum, Walser watched as the German cities he had known and loved were destroyed. The people and the places he wrote for disappeared or dead.

He died looking up at the sky, one hand on his heart, the other a handful of snow.

---

* See Susan Bernofksy's CLAIRVOYANT OF THE SMALL: THE LIFE OF ROBERT WALSER (New Haven, CT: Yale University Press, 2021)

MY FIRST WALK OUT OF 2025

I took the winding path to the top of the hill and—as I descended—a little boy was dancing towards the top. He dipped, as I watched him, into one of the tumuli (more or less exactly where King Penda of the FEN emerges from in the film) and cried: 'This doesn't feel real, but it is!'

*

JOSHUA BONNETTA
HERISAU SKETCHES (OCTOBER 8)

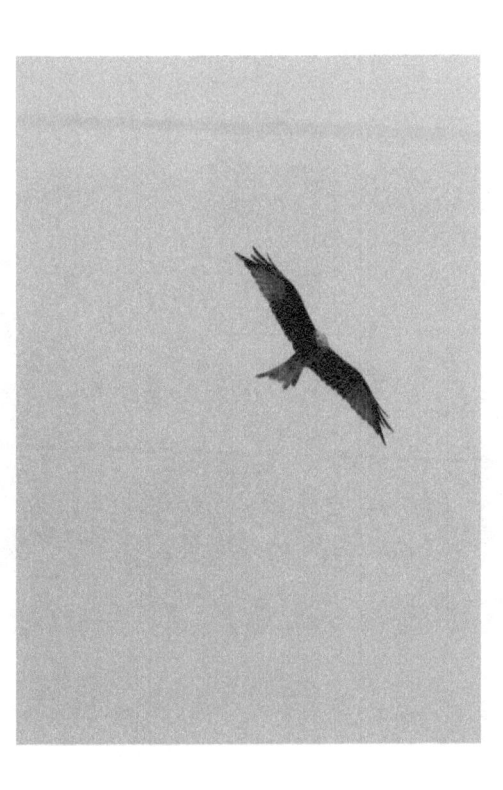

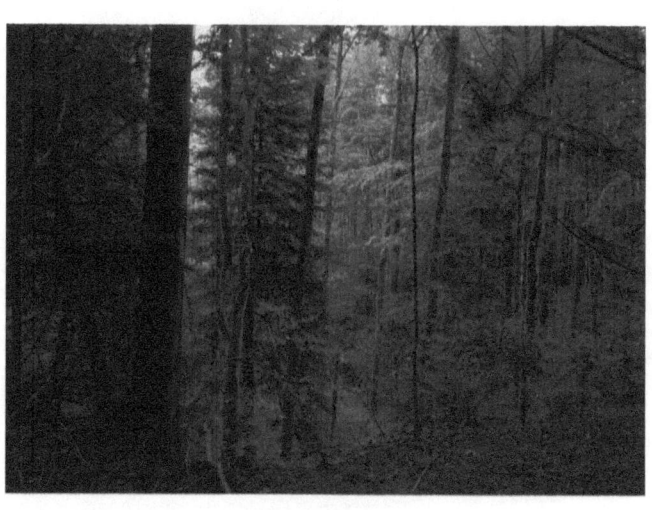

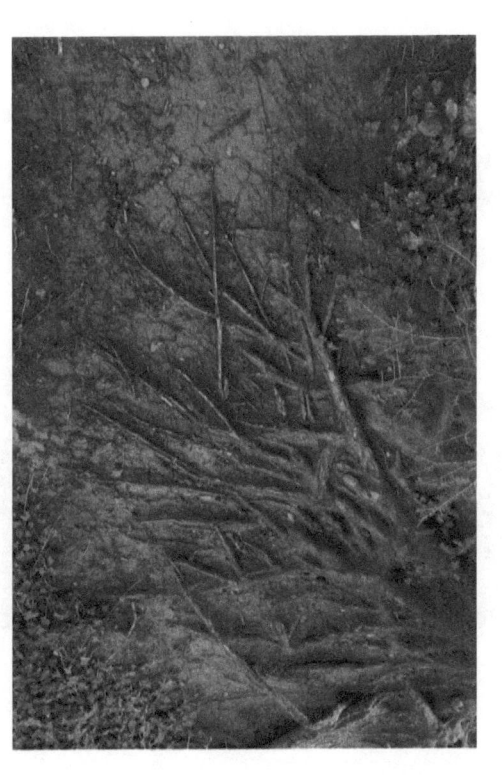

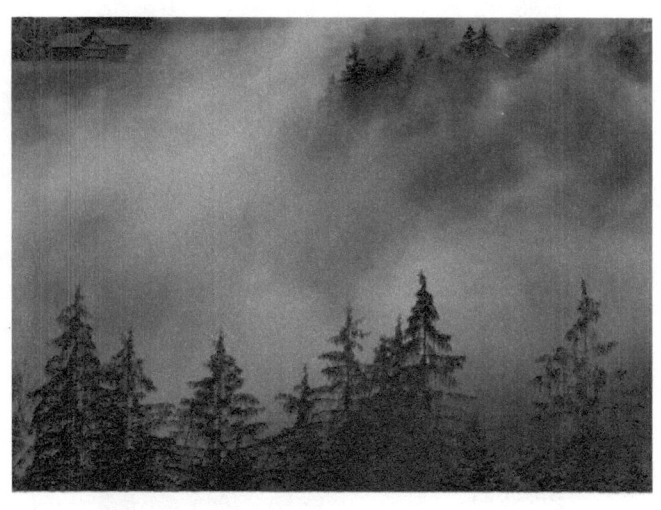

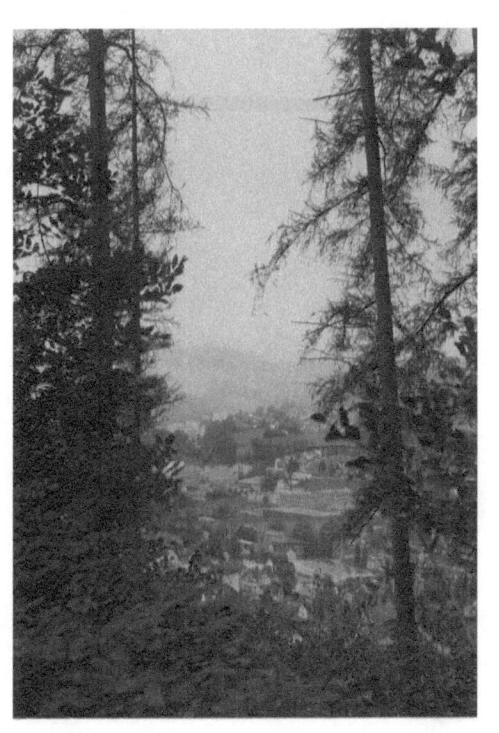

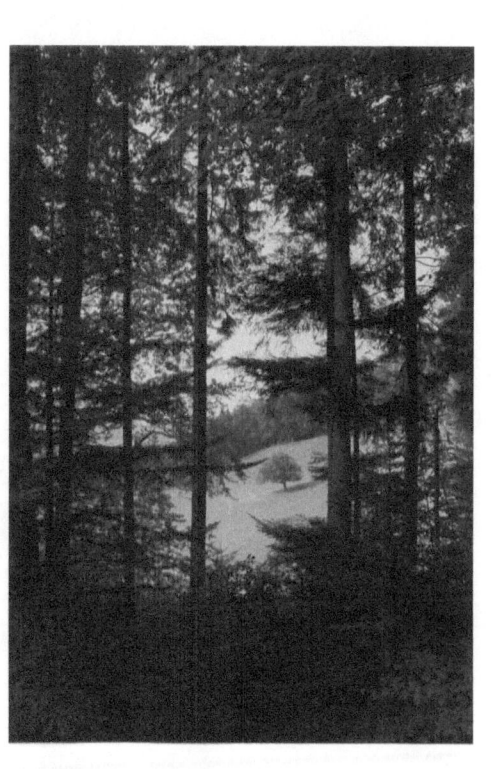

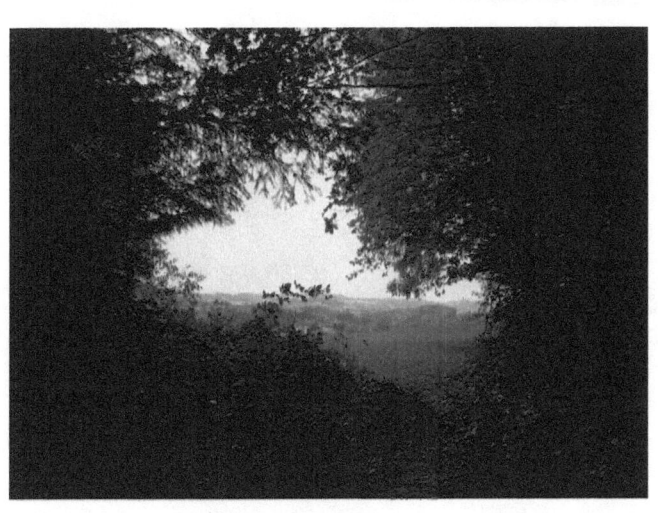

STANLEY SCHTINTER is the winner of nothing. He lives and works between the gutter and the stars.

GARETH EVANS is a London-based writer (when he does), film / walk / event producer, and host for hire.

JOSHUA BONNETTA is a Munich-based filmmaker and sound artist.

SNOW, ALWAYS SNOW

A Conversation between Stanley Schtinter & Gareth Evans
on the implications & associations relative to a film,
SCHNEEWITTCHEN
(S. Schtinter, 70m., 35mm, MMXXV)

Gareth Evans & Stanley Schtinter, © 2025.

SNOW, ALWAYS SNOW was first published in the United Kingdom by Tenement Press. SNOW, ALWAYS SNOW was edited by Dominic J. Jaeckle, and designed and typeset by Traven T. Croves (Matthew Stuart & Andrew Walsh-Lister).

Unless otherwise indicated, all illustrations and photography included in this volume are in the public domain, with the exception of stills excerpted from Schtinter's SCHNEEWITTCHEN (pp.V, XXXII, XLI), and reproductions of photographs by Joshua Bonnetta (pp.CXXVI, CXXVII, CXXVIII, CXXIX, CXXX, CXXXI, CXXXII, CXXXIII); works by Schtinter and Bonnetta appear courtesy of the artist(s), Schtinter, © 2025; Bonnetta, © 2025), Doi Toshitsura's 'Snow flowers' (pp. LXV, LXVI, LXVII, LXVIII, LXIX, LXX) are in the public domain. The spine text, 'Astral music, a moving picture, standing still,' is excerpted from Hanns Zichsler's essay, "Think of Me,' Whispered the Dust: Thoughts on the Images from the Churyumov-Gerasimenko Comet' (see also p.LXXXVII); an essay first published in Jean-Pierre Bibring & Hanns Zischler, *Comet: Photographs from the Rosetta Space Probe* (Paris: Éditions Xavier Barral, 2019 / London: Thames & Hudson, 2019), pp.199–209.

The rights of Gareth Evans and Stanley Schtinter to be identified
as authors of this work have been asserted in accordance with
Section 77 of the Copyright, Designs and Patents Act 1988. All
efforts to identify copyright and secure permissions have been
pursued where necessary and possible; fair dealing of works
is listed in Section 30a, Schedule 2 (2a) of the Copyright, Designs
and Patents Act 1988.

Tenement Press / Harry Caul 1, MMXXV
ISBN 978-1-917304-07-8

Printed and bound by Lulu.
Typeset in Arnhem Pro Blond.

Tenement Press is an occasional publisher of esoteric;
experimental,
accidental,
angular,
and interdisciplinary literatures.

The 'Harry Caul' series—a thread of feature-length interviews and exchanges between makers—is named for the precarious listener at the apex of Francis Ford Coppola's *The Conversation* (1973).

www.tenementpress.com
editors@tenementpress.com

www.ingramcontent.com/pod-product-compliance
Lightning Source LLC
Chambersburg PA
CBHW020440220526
45464CB00002B/787